Diary of a Country Carmelite

A Year in the Garden of Carmel

Also by the author:

Diary of a Country Mother
A Year Remembering Tim

DIARY OF A COUNTRY CARMELITE

A Year in the Garden of Carmel

by
Cynthia A. Montanaro, OCDS

Country Carmelite Books

Cover design Miriam Schroder
Interior design Nora Malone

To my Carmelite family:
St. Joseph Community, OCDS,
in Turners Falls, Massachusetts
and
to Suzie Andres, OCDS, in California and
Priscilla McCaffrey of Catholic
Media Apostolate in Connecticut,
whose interest and encouragement
helped give birth to this book

Contents

Diary of a Country Carmelite

A Year in the Garden of Carmel

Introduction

December 20, 2014

I have put off the outside chores long enough. The chickens *do* need feeding, after all, despite my desire to remain where it is warm. As always, once I am outside, the open-aired, calm beauty penetrates my soul. All is sepia-toned except for a few splotches of color here and there. The branches of the red twig dogwood, the mountain laurel leaves with the glossy red holly berries next to them. A few small birds dart about overhead.

The quiet is palpable as I walk to the barn, carefully stepping over some old piles of snow on the way. I slide the latch on the door, noticing the row of icicles on the edge of the barn roof and hearing the hens cackling an invitation when they are tipped off that food is imminent. There is beauty for all the senses if I can just be attuned.

Beauty of all sorts. Visible and invisible. Take the Liturgy of the Hours, for example. Today as we approach Christmas, we are invited to experience the great longing of the people of Israel for a Savior. The *O Antiphons*, those ancient words from the Old Testament, are saturated with this beauty. "*O Clavis David*" we hear on December 20th every year.

O key of David and scepter of Israel, what you open no one else can close again; what you close no one can open. O come to lead the captive from prison.

Diary of a Country Carmelite

Christ is the long-awaited opener of all doors, the One who leads Israel from its captivity and still today leads us from the prisons of our own worst selves.

There is much remembered beauty today, too. I go back in mind to this day in 2007 when I officially began my life as a Secular Carmelite. It was an evening ceremony and as the priest placed the squares of brown wool upon my shoulders, I was admitted into formation ... call it a spiritual training camp if you want ... of the Discalced Carmelite Order. We are ordinary laypeople, not priests (First Order) or nuns (Second Order), but simply husbands, wives or single folks who feel called to a deeper prayer life, a more faithful living out of the Gospel; a life offered as a gift to God for His praise and for the benefit of all those around us.

We "desire to live in the world and to walk in the light of the Gospel in the spirit of the Teresian Carmel and under the protection of the Blessed Virgin Mary."

It is a tall order, and in the period of formation when one leaves behind the pre-conceived expectations of the old days and delves deeper into the life of prayer ahead, there are new questions: "Is this what God wants of me?" and "Can I really be faithful to this life?"

It was a far cry from what was occupying my mind and heart a few years earlier. In December of 2005 I had just begun my first year of writing: *Diary of a Country Mother*, the journal I started six months after the death of our son, Tim. I was calm and at peace then, but still in a dark fog about where life would lead me next. Tim was the youngest of our four boys and the only one left at home. My life was all wrapped up in teaching him and in all the other cares of a mother, house-wife and head gardener on our seven-acre country "estate".

My year of writing was a Godsend. It gave me the grace and insight to dig deeper into the personhood of our son and into the profound meaning of his life and of Life itself. It reinforced my belief in a loving God whose comfort never wavers and who has left us with a

Church to guide and strengthen us in our days of "exile". My year of writing was also an occupation that bridged two periods of my life as I shifted course and was finally able to look ahead as well as behind.

Now I pick up my pen again to ponder other questions: those of vocation and purpose and faithfulness. Having found my path and having discovered that it is a road of great beauty and fulfillment, I wish to share with others the joy that I find in my life as a country *Carmelite*.

So, I invite you to travel along with me in this year of study and meditation as I prepare for my definitive profession in the Spring. You will learn what a Carmelite Secular is and what she isn't; just what kind of promises one makes and whether it is easy or difficult to live them out.

We will learn about all the Carmelite saints and blesseds, not just the "Big Three": St. Teresa of Jesus, St. John of the Cross and St. Thérèse of the Child Jesus. We will find out what distinguishes them from one another and see what each of them has to teach us as we move from one feast day to the next in the liturgical year.

We will explore the theme of contemplative prayer and come to understand the teachings of the saints on this topic. We might think we can understand how a cloistered monk or nun can "pray always" as the Gospel commands us, but how about one who is still "in the world"?

It will be a year of simple journeying as I am no theologian or expert in the field of Carmelite studies, just an average Catholic woman who is learning as she goes along and who carries in her knapsack a great desire to point out each vista along the way and to see that they are accessible to other seekers.

It will be a year of profound physical beauty, too, as we look at a sunset together, see the first spears of hosta push up through the soil and smell the damp leaves after a fall rain. This Carmelite lives in the country after all and each experience can bring food for meditation.

Diary of a Country Carmelite

I can't see all that the road ahead will bring in the coming year. I know of a few stops I'd like to make along the way, at least I have planned my trip to include them, but so often God has other routes for us to follow, as we all know only too well. With Him along as guide, though, the tramp will be a pilgrimage and the destination just the place of refreshment that he had planned for me from all eternity.

> Show us, then, O our good Master, some way in which we may live through this most dangerous warfare without frequent surprise. The best way that we can do this, daughters, is to use the love and fear given us by His Majesty. For love will make us quicken our steps, while fear will make us look where we are setting our feet so that we shall not fall on a road where there are so many obstacles. Along that road all living creatures must pass, and if we have these two things we shall certainly not be deceived. (St. Teresa of Avila, *The Way of Perfection*)

December 21, 2014

The snow is falling softly with big, clingy flakes clumping on the windshield as I buckle my seatbelt and head west into the hills on this 4th Sunday of Advent. The Visitation Sisters have a monastery about half an hour from home. It is situated on a hillside in a most picturesque valley. *Mont Deux Coeurs*, Mount of Two Hearts, draws me again this year to the annual program of Lessons and Carols.

In the quiet of the chapel as dusk approaches, we are an eager group—part audience and part congregation—that fills the small space as we listen to the nuns' voices along with the flute and organ and a few guest singers. The program captures so completely the beauty and longing of Advent. It is the *perfect* contemplative prelude to Christmas. My lists and wrappings are gladly set aside to ponder the eternal truth upon which all our celebrating is hinged.

On the drive back home in the cloak of evening dark, I have more time to consider the jumble of thoughts, readings and carols this day presented. The Office of Readings for the day gave a commentary on Luke by St. Ambrose. His topic was the Visitation (here again another *dear* conjunction of words in the event and the Congregation) and he finishes with these two thoughts:

> Let Mary's soul be in each of you to proclaim the greatness of the Lord. Let her spirit be in each to rejoice in the Lord. Christ has only one mother in the flesh, but we all bring forth Christ in faith.

and

> In another place we read: magnify the Lord with me. The Lord is magnified, not because the human voice can add anything to God but because he is magnified within us. Christ is the image of God, in whose likeness it was created and, in magnifying the image of God, the soul has a share in its greatness and is exalted.

Here, in these two thoughts are contained an entire feast of images—but also a deep reality. With Mary's soul in us we can bring forth Christ. What a thought! How the world needs this constant bringing forth. And further, with our right-ness and holy-ness we magnify God's image within us.

May I live this Christmas well, O Lord, so that I may bring forth the Word made flesh and image of the Father!

There are just a few days before Christmas but I know there will be ample opportunity to work on the "right and holy" part amid all the personalities and the acts of hospitality that crowd together during this season.

Diary of a Country Carmelite

December 28, 2014

My mother and father drove three hours south from their cozy log cabin in Upstate New York to spend the Christmas season with us. Mom and I baked and cooked together, with Dad ever ready for dishwashing, potato peeling or table setting. Christmas Mass was full of peace and beauty. The days celebrating with our son Paul, his wife, Jasmine, and their family brought that particular brand of joy that children and Christmas are famous for.

This morning, on the drive down the mountain to Mass the car is quiet. The weather has been mild for a change and there is no new snow to contend with, so Andy, driving, is lost in his own thoughts and prayers. I pray the Office of Readings in the back seat while my father reads the letters of Padre Pio and Mom peruses a book of meditations by Francis Fernandez.

Today is the feast of the Holy Family and we ponder the example of our three: Jesus, Mary and Joseph, in the home at Nazareth. I smile in the quiet car as I finish the Second Reading from a 1964 address by Pope Paul VI and think once again about how aptly the Office of Readings can prepare us for Holy Mass or be an echo of the day's liturgical readings and seasons if prayed after Mass.

Paul VI teaches us several lessons that we can learn from observing the life of the Holy Family. The first is the lesson of silence.

> The silence of Nazareth should teach us how to meditate in peace and quiet, to reflect on the deeply spiritual, and to be open to the voice of God's inner wisdom and the counsel of his true teachers. Nazareth can teach us the value of study and preparation, of meditation, of a well-ordered spiritual life, and of silent prayer that is known only to God.

The second lesson is Nazareth as a model of family life ... "*a community of love and sharing, beautiful for the problems it poses and the rewards it brings; in sum, the perfect setting for rearing children—and for this there is no substitute.*"

The value of work and the example of discipline is the third lesson that the Holy Father holds up for our inspection.

As I close my book I also think about the gift of my own family and how the faith of my parents has guided me and formed me: as a child with the concerns of everyday life, in my appreciation for hard work, in the choices I have made and in my own marriage and family life. What a blessing to have grown up in a faithful Catholic family.

Family life also prepares us for our vocation. Here we either learn how to imitate the love of our own parents or to avoid repeating a bad example if we have not had the privilege of a loving family. In the heart of the family we also begin to yearn for our own more intimate experience of family love if we are called to marriage. And here we can learn the generosity of self-giving that precedes every gift of a religious vocation.

But family love, even in a good family, is only a weak representation of the love of God for each of us. "*For God so loved the world that He sent his only begotten son*" (John 3:16) ... into a *family*.

Have a rejoicing heart, try to grow holy,
help one another, keep united, live in peace.
—Sing and make music to the Lord in your hearts.
(Responsory to Second Reading, Feast of the Holy Family)

January

It is very still on this cold Saturday morning as I head out to Andy's truck and crank up the heater. There is a prediction of snow and ice later on, but for now, the roads are clear as I head to Mass at Our Lady of the Blessed Sacrament Church in Westfield. Today is the feast of the Holy Name of Jesus, a feast which was added to the Church calendar in 1721 by Pope Innocent XIII, removed in 1969 when the liturgical calendar was revised, but then added back by Pope St. John Paul II.

For me, it is the end of a little "at home retreat" since I have been home alone for the past few days while Andy has been visiting his brothers and sister in the Syracuse area.

The church is full of Christmas beauty and its own sort of stillness this morning. I am grateful that this feast gives us another chance to meditate on the Incarnation and on the important place that a name can have, especially the name of Jesus.

Dear memories come to mind of sitting down with the boys when they were little and teaching them the importance of the second commandment.

Teach them to call on Jesus, Mary and Joseph as soon as they are able to lisp out; also the prayers like the "Our Father", the "Hail Mary" and other small prayers. How commendable it is to nourish the souls of your children, as you bring them up in the physical plane. (St. Kuriakos)

Today is also the feast day of a Carmelite priest who was canonized just this past November by Pope Francis. St. Kuriakos Elias of the Holy Family Chavara was born in Kerala, India in 1805, the son of a devout Catholic couple of the Syro-Malabar Church.

At the young age of 13 he entered the seminary and was ordained a priest in 1829. He had the great desire to retire to a quiet place and live the life of a hermit, but was dissuaded by his bishop who recognized the good that he could do for the people of Kerala.

The bishop was certainly correct! In 1855 he took vows as a Carmelite and founded an order for men, the Carmelites of Mary Immaculate, and for women, the Congregation of Mother of Carmel. St. Kuriakos began schools, a seminary, the first printing press, a house for the dying and destitute and was often preaching retreats to groups of lay people. Today there are over 3000 members of the Carmelites of Mary Immaculate, including 9 bishops, 1766 priests and 1200 brothers in formation. They serve not only in India but in 27 countries around the world. What great fruit from this one vocation!

St. Kuriakos offered a sacrifice of his own personal desires, the wish to withdraw from the active life to the purely contemplative, to obey his bishop who was inspired to offer counsel regarding his vocation. Maintaining a great life of prayer and interior recollection he sacrificed his own inclinations and accomplished the vocation God had in mind for him— the help and sanctification of the Church and the people of India.

While we are here on earth, prayer, even contemplation itself, cannot consist solely in the enjoyment of God; it must always be united with sacrifice, only thus is it true. Authentic prayer and contemplation incite the soul to generosity, disposing it to accept for God any labor or toil, and to give itself entirely to Him. (Fr. Gabriel of St. Mary Magdalen, OCD, *Divine Intimacy,* 59)

January 7, 2015

We celebrated Tim's Adoption Day today as we do on this day every year. A funny family tradition dictates that the menu includes pizza and eggnog. Once again, I offer my thanksgiving to God for bringing Tim into our family and for all the graces that accompanied his life and death.

Today marks the tenth celebration without him. I can hardly believe that so many years have passed.

I bring the eggnog and chocolate torte and some pizza toppings down to Westfield where, together with Tim's family, we happily and noisily prepare the feast. The grandchildren ask again for "Uncle Tim stories"—Oh, we have so many in the archives—and we simply and beautifully enjoy each other's company.

I made enough eggnog this year for our mechanic Gary, in memory of his own son Timothy. Big-hearted Tim is, no doubt, happy to share the spotlight.

I often "hear" Tim's famous sayings at various times and places. On January 7th this is the one that always comes to mind:

I guess God adopted all the people just like you guys adopted me. (Tim)

The meaning is clear: those who have the firstfruits of the spirit are groaning in expectation of the adoption of sons. This adoption of sons is that of the whole body of creation, when it will be as it were a son of God and see the divine, eternal goodness face to face. (from a letter by St. Ambrose, bishop)

Diary of a Country Carmelite

January 8, 2015

The thermometer read 6 below zero this morning! Thankfully the wind has settled down. Last night the howling was so loud that it was difficult to fall asleep, so I am especially glad for a reprieve.

Today and tomorrow we celebrate the feasts of two Carmelite saints who were European contemporaries. Despite disparate backgrounds they both rose to great prominence in their separate countries and made noble contributions to the cause of peace and to the sanctity of the people.

The first, St. Peter Thomas, was born in France at the beginning of the 14th century. His family were poor farm folk but they must have taught him the value of hard work, if his later life is any indication. Peter was a talented student but had to work to put himself through school by tutoring and teaching others. He became a professor at a Carmelite monastery and eventually entered the community himself, going on to further studies and then ordination to the priesthood.

He was a talented preacher and the way he had with words, coupled with his sanctity and sociability, made him one of those rare men who could move hearts. He preached at the Papal Court in Avignon, was an advisor to Popes Clement VI and Innocent VI and was sent as an emissary to emperors and on diplomatic missions to restore peace after conflicts. This "ideal Carmelite" was ordained Bishop of Patti in Sicily, served as Archbishop of Crete and Latin Patriarch of Constantinople. He accompanied a fleet of Crusaders, yet had the charity and humility to care for those suffering from the plague. He died in 1366.

There are two stories of Peter Thomas' particular devotion to Our Lady which have been passed down to us due to the close friendship of his biographer, Philip de Mezieres. (As a librarian, I also would like to acknowledge the great debt that we have to those who preserved this book so it can be of use to us 650 years later!)

When he was a young Carmelite and worried about the money needed to pay for his studies, Mary appeared to him with words of reassurance and the next day he was given enough money to continue. Then, later when he was in Avignon, Mary again became visible during prayer with more reassurance: "Have confidence, Peter, for the Carmelite Order will last until the end of the world. Elijah, its founder, has already obtained it a long time ago from my Son."

St. Andrew Corsini was born a few years before Peter Thomas in the city of Florence, Italy. Unlike Peter, he came from a wealthy, noble family, but fell into the sinful life that wealth and power can often induce. Somehow or the other, thanks to the tears and prayers of his mother, he had the grace to recognize his errors and thanked her and the Blessed Mother before entering the Carmelite monastery where he persevered despite many difficulties. He, too, was sent for further studies and earned a doctorate in theology. Later his talents also earned him the election as prior of his monastery and eventually, Bishop of Fiesole.

Like Peter, Andrew was entrusted with a diplomatic mission. Urban V appointed him mediator to settle a dispute between the Italian city-states of Bologna and Milan. Despite the polar opposites of the warring parties and their hotheaded personalities, he established peace.

As with all good Carmelites, St. Andrew Corsini was a true and devoted son of Mary. What sets him apart is the fact that he was known for miracles and conversions, even during his lifetime. He died in 1373 and is still beloved and called upon for aid in the city of Florence.

I wonder if Peter and Andrew, both bishops in Italy and both diplomats, ever met?

The stories of these two saints point out the truth that each of us is called to a vocation and mission that is particular to our own time and surroundings. With God's grace, we too can be teachers and diplomats, peacemakers and preachers. The stakes may not be as high or the notoriety as exalted as in Peter's and Andrew's times, but each one of us has our audience and theatre of action. With our eyes on Christ we can also bring with us a retinue of Christians who have heard our words and witnessed our example.

> Prayer is … a mine which is never exhausted …
> It is the root, the fountain,
> the mother of a thousand blessings. (St. Andrew Corsini)

January 17, 2015

It is another bitter cold day and the driveway has an inch of ice under a dusting of snow. I make it safely out to the car and am soon on a well-plowed road with no need to worry about the drive down the mountain.

I started taking the ornaments off the Christmas tree this morning. To make the job a little more cheerful I put on a CD of Christmas hymns, *Gaudete Mundi, Carols to the Newborn King,* sung by a choir of joyful nuns. One liturgical season put to bed as another begins.

As I drive along I think about that need to always bring forth Christ to the world as St. Ambrose had said. I carried the thought up the steps into the dark and silent church and in the tabernacle of my soul during Mass. Who needs to put Christmas away in the dark attic for another year?

As if to echo that thought, after Mass a friend who bears a strong resemblance to Santa Claus leaned over as if he had something important to say to me. With a twinkle in his eye, only two words were whispered … "Merry Christmas!"

What joy each and every moment of the day has in store when it is lived in the recollected presence of the Holy Trinity!

We live in a world which *does* have such a need of the continual bringing forth and proclaiming of Christ. In the past week there was a massacre in a magazine office, a hostage-taking in a grocery store, stories of abuse, the murder of innocents and personal pleas for prayers of intercession from friends and family. We are surrounded globally and locally by sin and horror, sickness and strife. The world is still in need of a Savior and largely sees Him not. If we are at all compassionate and concerned about our near neighbors and those across the ocean, then we search for a way to help.

What is my solution? What can I do on my icy road in my little country town? I am full of confidence and have a definite plan of attack. I pull out my breviary and pray, united with a host of other dedicated souls. I give my day to fighting with the ancient prayer of the Psalms and with the surety that I am moving mountains of division and healing illnesses and binding wounds. All with the union of my prayer … all of us together praising God through the Liturgy of the Hours, assembling for Holy Mass and listening to every call of duty in the course of the day.

Secular Carmelites have the duty to bring forth Christ to the world by faithfulness to our obligations. Every day we pray Lauds (Morning Prayer) and Vespers (Evening Prayer) of the Liturgy of the Hours, which is also called the Divine Office or the Breviary. Before bed we pray Compline, (Night Prayer) as we mull over the day's success and failures and beg God's watchfulness as we sleep. Sandwiched in between our daily tasks we put everything aside for 30 minutes of mental prayer, at least 15 minutes spiritual reading and, when we are able, present ourselves in front of the altar for daily Mass, the summit and source of Catholic worship.

When we are not actively involved in prayer, we can still be present before the throne of God by maintaining an actual awareness of His presence, as St. Teresa reminds us. "We need no wings to go in search of Him, but have only to find a place where we can be alone and look upon Him present within us."

Diary of a Country Carmelite

I can wash dishes, shovel snow, vacuum up pine needles and write a letter, shop for groceries and put gas in the car while living in the presence of God. So simple and yet, so sublime!

I put on my "battle fatigues" of prayer as I don my scapular in the morning, becoming an invisible warrior for truth, goodness and peace with every breath and every step.

As if to echo the need for my diligence, I see an ambulance heading down our icy road. It pulls in the driveway at the horse farm next door. Later I will go and see if I can be of help. For now, though, I pick up my breviary and pray the Office of Readings, certain that I am calling on the "big guns" and bringing forth Christ for my neighbor Joey who, I find out later, has just fallen on the ice.

Spirit of truth and love,
Life-giving holy dove,
Speed on your flight;
Move on the water's face,
Bearing the lamp of grace,
And in earth's darkest place
Let there be light.
(John Marriott, 1780-1825, ad. by Anthony G. Petti, Hymn from the Office of Readings, Wednesday, Week 1)

I close my eyes, and while my lips murmur the words of
    the Breviary which I know by heart, I leave behind
    their literal meaning,
and feel that I am in that endless land where the Church,
militant and pilgrim, passes, walking towards the prom-
    ised fatherland.
I breathe with the Church in the same light by day, the
    same darkness by night.
I see on every side of me the forces of evil that beset
    and assail Her;

I find myself in the midst of Her battles and victories,
Her prayers of anguish and Her songs of triumph,
in the midst of the oppression of prisoners,
the groans of the dying, the rejoicing of the armies and
   captains victorious.
I find myself in their midst, but not as a passive spectator;
nay rather, as one whose vigilance and skill,
whose strength and courage can bear a decisive weight
on the outcome of the struggle between good and evil,
and upon the eternal destinies of individual men and of the
   multitude.
(Blessed Cardinal Ildefonso Schuster, Archbishop of Milan,
   1929-1954)

January 27, 2015

Every snow day seems to be a day set apart in one way or another.
Our usual activities are modified, plans are cancelled and the mold of
the ordinary is changed in subtle ways ... or sometimes even greatly.

Yesterday we heard dire predictions that a blizzard of mammoth
proportions was making its way toward the northeast and that we
had all better be prepared. My pantry was pretty well-stocked, so I
just picked up some lamp oil at the hardware store in case we lost
electricity, baked an extra loaf of bread and waited.

Despite a declared "state of emergency" and a local travel ban,
we only saw 6" of snow, while points east had several feet. So, Andy
and I enjoyed a day off with none of the stress of getting to work
over slippery roads.

I used my bonus day to finish painting the kitchen and enjoyed
Andy's company in the middle of the week. I also had some leisure

to learn a little more about today's Carmelite saint, Henry de Osso y Cervello.

St. Henry was born in Spain in the middle of the 19th century, but like his Carmelite confreres, Peter Thomas in France and Andrew Corsini in Italy, he had a significant impact on the people and culture of his era.

By all reports, Henry was a devout child who responded with fervor to God's pull, even at an early age. He entered the seminary at Tortosa, later studied in Barcelona and was ordained to the priesthood in 1867. He was another one of those priests whose personality and demeanor naturally attracted people; traits which Henry used to great advantage in his ministry. He gave retreats to children and adults, teaching people the elements of prayer and encouraging them in virtue.

Besides his preaching he wrote numerous books and pamphlets and gave books away whenever he saw a need. St. Henry founded an order of nuns, the Society of St. Teresa, and helped bring the Discalced Carmelites to Tortosa where they opened a monastery. He founded centers for catechesis and began the Teresian Apostolic Movement to instruct children in the Teresian method of prayer and started an association for older men, too.

This is our main endeavor: to think, to feel, to love as Christ Jesus, to act and to speak as He—in a word to conform our whole life to Christ's.

Ever serene in the face of difficulties and possessing a great confidence in God's providential aid, Henry taught the virtuous life by example. He died in 1896 and was beatified in 1979 by Pope St. John Paul II who later canonized him in 1993.

Each saint who has gone before us has much to teach. Meditating on their lives and their fidelity to grace encourages me to keep striving and not to give in to discouragement. What's more, I am making the acquaintance of a whole cadre of new masters in the spiritual life whom I can call upon for help in a blizzard or in the summer's heat—all my brothers and sisters in Carmel who are encouraging that conformity to Christ.

> I will live, sleep, speak, listen, work, suffer—I will do every-thing, I will suffer everything in union with Jesus, with the same divine intention and sentiments that Jesus had and with which he suffered. Which is what Jesus wants of me. Whoever does this—and all of us are called to do it—will live in this life the life of the world to come and will be transformed into Jesus, able to say with St. Paul: "I live, no longer I, but Christ lives in me." (St. Henry de Osso y Cervello)

February

February 1, 2015

Ah, blessed relief! One more winter month is behind us and just two more to go! Some of you will know exactly what I mean when I write the words, "cabin fever." For the rest of you who live in temperate climates or with mild, short winters, here's the scenario: repeated days, weeks and months of bitter cold, days of snow, end on end, a dearth of light and bright sun. It takes a cumulative toll, too. Those of us suffering can get a little grumpy or genuinely irritable and sometimes even a little crazy. That's my excuse anyway!

Without a plan or even a nod to Andy, who was away visiting his siblings after Christmas, I pulled a little corner of loose wallpaper near the doorway in the kitchen. By the time he got home several days later, the job was almost finished and there was no hiding the stained wallboard that needed spackling and the disorder all around.

Perhaps you could chalk up my impetuous act to a fit of "cabin fever", or as I explained to Andy—equal parts of temptation and inspiration. Either way the deed was done!

To understand the complexity of the situation, I must admit to you that we are a color-challenged couple. I knew that before I could finish the kitchen makeover we would have to postulate and negotiate with periods of intense discussion: another skirmish in the "paint wars".

Diary of a Country Carmelite

I love color and play with it regularly in the garden, arranging flowers, piecing quilts and decorating the house. I wouldn't say that I am overly bold, though. I use lots of neutral colors to balance the effect.

Andy, on the other hand, is what I call a "color fundamentalist". In his mind, there are certain colors that go together and others that don't. He listened to my idea of the color scheme and just couldn't see it. I'll spare you the details of our ensuing conversations.

Of course, we always cool down after an intense "discussion" and apologize for crossing the lines of charity, but the whole ordeal pointed out to me only too clearly how attached *I* was to my own opinion.

Like many others who are on the path of the virtuous life, I had made a point of practicing detachment over the years. Having children in the house helps, too. Broken glasses and teapots, flowers run over by the lawn mower, tic-tac-toe games scratched into antique furniture. All the disorder of family life helps to put *things* into perspective. Taking everything in stride is not only good for cultivating a peaceful demeanor, it is a necessity for our prayer life.

When we are too attached to the things in our life there is hardly any room for God. Yes, we do need a furnished house and all the dishes, books, clothes and tools that go along with it, but we need to use them all in a detached way, always ready to give up that extra coat, a particular book or even a treasured piece of furniture when we see a need.

We can be just as attached to our own opinion and ideas, though. If I am truly trying to move forward in that life of virtue, that striving for perfection, I must work even harder to acquiesce and give up my stubbornly-held color preferences.

Peace will reign, I'll grow in humility and most of all, I'll be able to hear that still, small voice of Love that whispers to me.

It is quite a Carmelite endeavor, too. Here is our Holy Mother, Teresa, showing us the way:

O blessed detachment from all that is mean and perishable, to what a sublime state will you not raise me? You love me, my God, and for those who love You, Your love is no insignificant thing! Why, then should I not return Your love with all my strength? It would really be a happy exchange, O My God, giving You my love and receiving Yours. I know indeed that You can do everything, and that I can do only what You enable me to do. But what do I do for You, my Lord and Creator? I make some feeble resolutions which really amount to nothing. But if You wish me to gain everything by this nothing, I shall not be so foolish as not to listen to You! (*The Way of Perfection*, 16)

Now, with the kitchen freshly painted and a trip to the Confessional behind me, I can move a little farther along the path of self-knowledge towards the One who waits for me with open arms.

February 9, 2015

It's snowing again! As I looked out the kitchen window this morning, I could see the snow piling up higher and higher. It hasn't quite reached the bottom of the swing suspended from the sugar maple out front, but it is slowly inching upwards. Schools are closed again on this Monday morning and Andy is home from work. Another day to put aside my normal schedule and tackle a project. Today it will be cleaning out the sewing room.

The day's prayer is always stable, though, and grounds me in the interior life that is the core of my days ... even as I sort and file. Today after my early morning mental prayer and Morning Prayer from the Divine Office, I check my email and find, with joy, that there is a message from our son, Fr. Tom, in Rome.

Diary of a Country Carmelite

We had our monthly phone call with Tom last week and he told us about the gathering of all the priests and religious of Rome for a Mass at St. Peter's Basilica for the feast of the Presentation, Candlemas Day, on February 2nd. He was looking forward to concelebrating Mass with our Holy Father, Pope Francis.

Since that phone conversation I have been thinking about the debt that we owe to our Catholic priests, to the religious brothers and sisters and to the consecrated men and women who have all given their lives in service to God and for the good of souls. In this year dedicated to Consecrated Life it was a particularly momentous Mass at St. Peter's and I had asked Fr. Tom to send me his impressions and thoughts after concelebrating. He told me today:

> The Mass on the 2nd was very beautiful—I reflected at the beginning what the definitive moment of encounter of Our Lord will be like when the Bridegroom comes ... as all the religious had their candles lit. The Pope passed me by, by a couple of feet—and praying all together for the renewal of religious life was a grace. There are so many graces that it takes a while to digest it all, as you can imagine.

It is not always an easy life, separated from family, burdened with work and at times, with misunderstandings and discouragement, enduring physical and spiritual hardships and with few of the pleasures we lay folk take for granted.

As Carmelites we have the particular obligation to pray for priests at the command of our Holy Mother, St. Teresa of Jesus. Distraught over the loss of souls at the time of the Protestant Reformation, she instructed her nuns to dedicate themselves to praying for priests as she was certain of the immense good that a holy preacher could accomplish.

> All my longing was and still is that since He has so many enemies and so few friends that these few friends be good ones.

As a result I resolved to do the little that was in my power; that is, to follow the evangelical counsels as perfectly as I could and strive that these few persons who live here do the same. I did this trusting in the goodness of God, who never fails to help anyone who is determined to give up everything for Him. My trust was that if these Sisters matched the ideal my desires had set for them, my faults would not have much strength in the midst of so many virtues; and I could thereby please the Lord in some way. Since we would all be occupied in prayer for those who are the defenders of the Church and for preachers and for learned men who protect her from attack, we could help as much as possible this Lord of mine who is so roughly treated by those for whom He has done so much good ... (*The Way of Perfection*, 1:2).

St. Thérèse of the Child Jesus echoed this thought as well.

Behold, Our Lord, the mission You entrusted to me, to contribute by prayer and sacrifice to the formation of evangelical workers who will save millions of souls and whose mother I shall be. (*Letters*, 114)

Where would we be without holy priests? No Mass, no sacraments, no one to usher us into the family of God or out of this world and into His arms. No one to forgive our sins and bring us back from our places of debasement. No one to bring Christ to each of us in our needy world.

We all have a solemn obligation to pray for vocations to the priesthood and for the holiness of our priests. It's not just a duty for the cloistered nuns. Before Fr. Tom's ordination I found a document on the website of the Congregation for the Clergy entitled, "*Adoration, Reparation, Spiritual Motherhood for Priests*". In less than forty pages it told the stories of a dozen women, some mothers, some consecrated religious, and in one instance, even a whole town of women, who had given their lives in prayer and sacrifice for priests. Several of the priests and bishops became aware of those who were sacrificing themselves for the efficacy of their work but often they remained anonymous in this life. The little booklet was filled with photographs and offered a moving exposition of both the need and the remedy. I printed it from my computer and passed on the link to others, all the while wishing it were available in print.

Fast forward several years ... Fr. Thomas has been ordained in a ceremony unrivaled in my experience in the Basilica of St. John Lateran in Rome with 48 of his brothers. Just being in Rome was amazing enough, but here was this son of ours being anointed to carry on the work Christ left for His Church. I was awestruck!

That day I realized more completely the solemn obligation that I have, but really that we all share, to give our lives in prayer and sacrifice for these priests—for all my priest-sons.

When we returned home from Rome and from a perfect week in the Holy Land with Fr. Tom, I copied out the address of the cardinal who headed the Congregation of the Clergy, intending to write to him and ask that the little book be published. It must have ended up at the bottom of one pile or another because I never wrote that letter.

God heard my plea, though, and surely those of many others, for when I spoke with the publisher shortly before *Diary of a Country Mother* came out in print, he told me he wanted to place a little advertisement on the last page of the book. The title he said, was, *Adoration, Reparation, Spiritual Motherhood for Priests*. Ah!

Behind and prior to every vocation to the priesthood or the consecrated life is always someone's powerful and intense prayer; a grandmother's, a grandfather's, a mother's, a father's, a community's.... This is why Jesus said: "Pray to the Lord of the harvest", that is God the Father, "that he might send workers for the harvest!" (Matthew 9:38) Vocations are born in prayer; and only in prayer can they persevere and bear fruit. (Pope Francis, Good Shepherd Sunday, April 21, 2013)

February 13, 2015

The circumstances of our days can vary so much from one day to the next or even one moment to another. Despite the seeming monotony of another endless windy day, this one will be unique and unrepeatable, despite the same beginning, the same wind, the same painful, bitter cold and the same work around the house.

A day begun in prayer is already sanctified and so, resting in God's peace I can be ready to go about my day with what I had planned—writing some letters, feeding the chickens, and washing dishes, or be ready to change those plans when the phone rings and I need to make a "house call" to a friend in need.

For Brother Lawrence of the Resurrection, a lay Carmelite brother living in a monastery in France in the 17th century, his prayer and his work in the kitchen preparing meals and washing up were one and the same. His spiritual life was spent "Practicing the Presence of God", which for him meant that he could always be with God, whether he was in church or not, whether it was a time of prayer or a time to work.

We can make our hearts an oratory where we can withdraw from time to time to converse with him there, gently, humbly, and lovingly. Everyone is capable of these conversations with God, some more, some less. He knows what we can do. (Brother Lawrence, *Practice of the Presence of God*)

Peace reigns in the soul that practices this presence, so no matter where I am or what I am doing—visiting a friend with a sick goat, kneeling at Mass or driving in the car when the heater suddenly stops—I am not distraught or overly concerned. Then every moment of the day is a prayer. The wind can blow; it can howl around me with fury. No matter. My roots are buried deep in the heart of Christ who is my stability and peace.

> Every person needs a "center" in his life, a source of truth and goodness to draw from in the flux of the different situations of everyday life and its toil. Every one of us, when he pauses for a moment of silence, needs to feel not only the beating of his own heart, but more deeply, the beating of a trustworthy presence perceptible to the senses of faith and yet more real: the presence of Christ, heart of the world. (Benedict XVI, Angelus, June 1, 2008)

February 20, 2015

The weather always seems to be a handy topic of conversation. We are all cold and a little weary of being blown about by the roaring wind and it gives us a sense of solidarity to share our trials with one another. Such was the common thread of conversation at the library yesterday.

We still have the brutal wind today and when a gust blows across the top of the snow in the back it reminds me of a rushing stream plunging over a waterfall.

Our town historical society is hosting a pot-luck dinner tonight so we will all, no doubt, start off comparing notes about the cold, snow and wind at first and then veer off to the topic of frozen water pipes. It's "Italy Night", though, so eventually we will help ourselves to plates of spaghetti and meatballs and listen to the travel stories of our neighbors who have been to Italy.

We have our own story to tell tonight and Andy has been selecting photos from our trip to Rome for Fr. Tom's ordination. As I looked over the pictures on the computer this morning, a word came to mind that accurately described the way I felt upon seeing the architectural beauties all about me—"*Stendhalismo*"! The word was coined after the 19th-century French author, Stendhal, visited Florence for the first time. He was overwhelmed and even physically light-headed and dizzy at the grandeur and beauty that he saw before him.

It's the same way for many visitors to Rome—centuries worth of architecture, sculpture and paintings at every point of the compass and around every bend of the road. It is hard to take it all in and appreciate it properly.

To go deeper, though, beyond what the senses are feeding the brain, we must consider the inspiration for the marble altars, gleaming columns, alabaster statues, and paintings that take one's breath away, second after second. The love of a Father, the monumental sacrifice of a Son, the gifts and inspiration of the Spirit.

Oh, that we could swoon with *Stendhalismo* over God's unrepeatable generosity and unparalleled gifts to us!

In a world that too often stops at the evidence of the senses, we have our work cut out for us: to make the deeper beauty visible to the gawkers. Beauty is a great draw, though, and it *can* be the starting point for an exchange of ideas that helps to open up that unseen world that is just under the surface.

Authentic beauty, however, unlocks the yearning of the human heart, the profound desire to know, to love, to go towards the Other, to reach for the Beyond. (Benedict XVI, Meeting with Artists, November 21, 2009)

Beauty is both ancient and new: we are at once surprised and comforted by its presence. Beauty exists in a sphere beyond time. And so beautiful things expose us to the timelessness of eternity.

That is why beauty matters in an eternal sense. Beauty was part of God's creative plan in the beginning, and it is just as much a part of his redemptive plan now. God has placed the desire for beauty within our hearts, and he uses that desire to lead us back to himself. (Bishop James. D. Conley, STL, "*Ever Ancient, Ever New: The Role of Beauty in the Restoration of Catholic Culture*," Crisis Magazine, 2013, based on an address to Catholic Answers Conference 9-2013)

February 25, 2015

A week ago my granddaughter, Isabella, and I made our way down the hills to the noon Mass on Ash Wednesday. It was school vacation week and I had the great delight of her company for several days. How easy it was to slip back into the mode of teacher as we talked about Lent, ashes and penance.

In our humanity there is always some degree of hesitation in embracing the penance of Lent. Though perhaps we have advanced along the road of self-denial since last Lent, we all know that it is time to begin once again—*Nunc Coepi*—to climb to another plateau in the spiritual life.

If we are to follow the admonition of Christ: "If anyone wishes to come after me, let him deny himself, and take up his cross, and follow me" (Mt. 16:24), we must have a great generosity of spirit, ready to make a gift of our own will. The road that follows behind Christ is, truly, a narrow path and we must give Him the gift of our selfish will, ever ready to indulge in appetites that satisfy our cravings for particular foods, distracting entertainments and bodily comforts.

The law of Lent is the law of Carmel! As Christ entered the desert for forty days to seek the Father in prayer, so we, as Carmelites, work, not just during Lent, but always, to silence the appetites, bear difficulties without complaint and accept with joy the trials that each day will bring.

We put our whole self into this work not because these practices are ends in themselves, but because we follow Jesus into the life of prayer and

> the efficacy of prayer depends especially on the degree of sanctity of the soul who makes it. (Fr. Marie Eugene, OCD, *I Want to See God*)

We are all a little rusty in complying … perhaps it has become hard to call a stop to the feasting of the Christmas season … but the dry grit of the ashes marks us, once again, as pilgrims on the path of asceticism, one of a great army of Christians plodding along behind Christ, whose life and suffering and death have won for us the hope of eternal life.

Fr. Gabriel of St. Mary Magdalen, OCD, holds up the example of our Carmelite saints to encourage us along the way:

> It was in this sense that St. Teresa Margaret of the Heart of Jesus resolved "not to let a single occasion for suffering escape, as far as she was able—and always in silence between God and herself." In fact she made every effort "to find at each moment some occasion for suffering or bodily pain, so as never to satisfy the slightest appetite or desire, and she sought ways to make even what was necessary, painful and wearying to her body" (*Spirituality of St. Teresa Margaret of the Heart of Jesus*). Her ardent love for God found an outlet in this generous, untiring exercise of mortification.
>
> Using a different expression, St Thérèse of the Child Jesus called this practice "scattering flowers," that is, profiting from

every least opportunity to suffer in order to give God a proof of her love. Knowing that the value of mortification depends upon the generosity of the dispositions with which it is done, the Saint said, "I shall always sing, even should my flowers be gathered from the midst of thorns" (*Story of a Soul*, 13). (Fr. Gabriel of St. Mary Magdalen, OCD, *Divine Intimacy*, 96)

Another Lent, another opportunity for generosity. May the mark of Your grace upon my forehead, Lord, be a reminder that, despite my weakness, I will have Your help along the road.

March

March 6, 2015

In our family, March seems to be the pre-eminent birthday month. In the course of these 31 days we celebrate with a son, a daughter-in-law, three grandsons and my mother. Then add on two nephews, a niece, two brothers-in-law and a sister-in-law as we move into the extended family, and you get a bigger, more complete picture of our March activity. I must dig deep into my reserves of creativity to come up with ideas for presents and will spend not a little time in the kitchen preparing culinary tokens of affection.

This morning I made oatmeal chocolate-chip cookies to mail to Alex in Alabama and delighted in the scents of lemon, garlic and olive oil as I made a dish of white bean dip to bring to our daughter-in-law Jasmine's birthday dinner tonight. We celebrate each person's birth and offer thanksgiving to the God of life for them, their talents and their unrepeatable personalities. And we thank God for placing us in a family. What joy!

As I work in the kitchen, I also think about the other families we belong to. High on my list is my Carmelite community. As lay people we each have our own families, but as Secular Carmelites we have been formed into another type of family. The "elders" help teach the newer members, give advice and open up the treasures that are inside the Carmelite family chest. Our Rule and its obligations, our saints and their wisdom, the beauty of this particular path that has been marked out for us. As in any other family, we pray for one another, too. A quick email or phone call can reach everyone in an instant and have us begging God on behalf of a sick son or daughter, a dying uncle or a befuddled teen. That's what families do. When we become part of a spiritual family the ties of our brotherhood are strong bonds that unite us in a common purpose, a common identity and a common endeavor.

> O, my God! I ask thee for myself and for those whom I hold dear, the grace to fulfill perfectly Thy Holy Will, to accept for love of Thee the joys and sorrows of this passing life, so that we may one day be united together in Heaven for all Eternity. Amen. (Morning Prayer by St. Thérèse)

As some of us prepare for professions next month, we read and ponder these words and give humble thanks to God, Father, Son and Spirit, who in the beauty and mystery of the Communion of Saints has called us into this family of love.

March 11, 2015

O glorious sun and warmth! We have been blessed with several days of warm weather—temperatures in the high forties and low fifties—and the snow is finally beginning to melt. There are puddles everywhere and the so-welcome sounds of dripping from the trees and gutters. It is always amusing to watch spirits lift when this happens in the spring. Dour faces are transformed and we hear light-hearted conversations about the weather at long last.

It is also tax season and Andy has been poring over forms and assembling documents. Once again it is time to officially define myself. That little blank line next to my signature awaits an answer. *Occupation?*

For years I have dallied about with indecision, somewhat humorously, trying to find the title that fits me best. "Housewife" is apt, but it is also saddled with the baggage of feminist disdain. And as I am not married to my house I have gone with "wife and mother" some years and, when busy homeschooling, have labeled myself, "teacher". Other years I tried on "librarian", but a little part-time job hardly makes that my occupation. For the past few years I could honestly have entered "writer", but then wonder: does that assume one is making money at an occupation?

This year, I almost decided on "Carmelite", but thought that would definitely confuse some poor revenuer.

All this linguistic see-sawing gets me thinking, about my life and my *vocation*, as opposed to my *occupation*.

I *am* occupied with caring for my family, keeping the house tidy and presentable, washing clothes and dishes, filling the cupboards and fixing the food that we eat … clearing paths in the winter and digging in the garden when the snow finally melts. Pretty ordinary stuff. Reflection and writing when things are quiet, covering and displaying books several afternoons a week. There is a great dignity in honest work well done, though, and I am happy to have this great variety of work to do.

It provides a certain parameter around my activity but it does not *define* me.

My unseen and interior life, my reason for being, gets to the heart of the matter and to my true dignity. I have a mission and a vocation that have been chosen for me and my talents and particular gifts. I am a collaborator on a global field with a host of others, a few that I know, but most I will never meet. Yet, we all work together in a massive network of cooperation.

Diary of a Country Carmelite

Our days are filled with the praise of God and a deep thanksgiving for the abundance that He has given us. We gather in small groups around an altar, as we are able, we pray at home and on our travels and we give every moment back as a gift of honor and petition with love.

Our faithfulness eases the pain of a dying grandmother, consoles a lonely teenager, strengthens an unemployed father and helps guide the hands of a surgeon. It is the life-blood of the Church, the consolation of priests and the hope of a world gone amuck. We press on, not knowing for whom we pray and not seeing results. There is no more important work in all the world!

Herein lies my dignity and worth.

What is the center and source of the life of the Church? The Host in the tabernacle, the little, silent Host, the praying Host, the loving Host. The apostles preach, but from the tabernacles of the world come forth rays of divine light, parts of the sun of love, which touch and enlighten souls. Be a praying and loving host, and you will send forth rays like the Host and God will give you all those who "voyage" with you, your neighbors, all those whom you love and whose salvation you ardently desire.

He needs truly loving souls, true hosts, truly transformed into Him by love. He needs such souls in order to save men.

You see, the world seems to run to its destruction, yet I am not a pessimist. Why? Because I think that today there are more souls than ever in cloisters and also in the world, entirely given to Jesus in complete confidence and total abandonment, without anything which distinguishes them from others, hidden like the Nazarene. (Jean C.J. d'Elbée, *I Believe in Love*)

So, in the end, it matters not one iota the "occupation" I mark on that black line. *I know my vocation.*

March 19, 2015

Today, which dawns sunny and windy, is a banner day in the liturgical year and in our family: the culmination of our novena to St. Joseph. For nine days we have been praying to Joseph and Fr. Tom has been offering a novena of Masses for our intentions. St. Joseph has always been our family's patron, especially when Andy needed to find a job, when we were looking for a house or apartment or when contemplating an important family decision.

Some saints are patrons to one or two classes of people, protectors of a town or country, but St. Joseph has a list as long as my arm. He is the patron of fathers, families, virgins, workers, expectant mothers, travelers, immigrants, craftsmen and engineers and the official protector of a slew of cities and countries. At the top of the list, we find him as patron of the Universal Church and of a happy death. He also happens to be the Protector of the Carmelite Order.

The just man, the one chosen by God to protect Mary and to be the earthly foster father of Christ, was the protector of this little family amid all the momentous trials that awaited them and also the one to see them through all the little crises common to any family. Joseph, who was familiar enough with listening in prayer, was able to recognize the angel's advice and warnings: *"Do not be afraid to take Mary.... Take the child and his mother and flee.... Return to Nazareth.... Withdraw into Galilee."*

For St. Teresa, St. Joseph was always her advocate in any large or small need. Her monasteries were all named for him or dedicated to him and she instructed her sisters to foster this devotion.

I have never known anyone to be truly devoted to you and render you particular services who did not notably advance

Diary of a Country Carmelite

in virtue, for you give very real help to souls who commend themselves to you. I have clearly seen that your help has always been greater than I could have hoped for. I do not remember that I have ever asked anything of you which you failed to grant. The Lord wishes to teach us that He himself was subject to you on earth (for being His guardian and being called His father, you could command Him), just so in heaven He still does all that you ask. (Teresa of Jesus, *Life*, 6)

The illustrious St. Joseph is also our model and teacher *par excellence* in the method and practice of prayer. He lived in intimate union with Jesus, son of the Father, and Mary, the holy one. He can direct us to them and provide for us the path to follow. Imitating his supreme calm in adversity and his unwavering confidence and trust in God's providence, we can move from superficial prayer to the deep, contemplative prayer of the particular friends of God; prayer that is as faithful in a comfortable home as it is in exile, in bounty as in want, in life as in the moment of death.

If anyone cannot find a master to teach him how to pray, let him take you as his master and he will not go astray. (Teresa of Jesus, *Life*, 6)

How is it that St. Joseph does this?

Joseph's prayer becomes contemplative precisely because Jesus— in the womb, as a child, as a boy, as a young man, as a partner in labor—is present to him. This presence propels Joseph ever more toward the Father, whom Joseph has come to love above all else. The ever increasing intimate union of Joseph's life with the life of the Father is the gift Mary and her child bring to this man of humble heart. Joseph's prayer is "the prayer of the child of God" (CCC 2712). It is a "gaze of faith, fixed on Jesus" (CCC 2715). (Fr. Gary Caster, *Joseph, The Man Who Raised Jesus*)

As I take the fragrant loaves, *Pane di San Giuseppe*, from the oven I inhale the pungent scent of anise and chuckle over the traditional shape of the bread, formed to resemble a patriarch's beard. When I deliver the bread today, I will pray that those who eat it will "go to Joseph" as we have always done in any necessity and with great confidence.

I pray that they will imitate his quiet, hidden life, model his simple, but perfect way of combining the active and contemplative life. For those of us who live in the world, beset by trials and tribulations, temptations and burdens, so much depends upon it.

O, St. Joseph, how much I love you! How much good it does me to think of your humble, simple life! Like us, you lived by faith. I contemplate you in the little house at Nazareth, near Jesus and Mary, busy working for them. I see you using the plane, and then wiping your forehead from time to time, and hurrying to finish the work on time for your customers. Although you lived with the Son of God, your life was very ordinary, for Jesus did not perform any useless miracles. Everything in your life was just as it is in ours. And how many sorrows, fatigues and dangers! Oh! how astonished we should be if we knew all that you suffered! (St. Thérèse of the Child Jesus, *Counsels and Souvenirs*)

March 25, 2015

We have this wonderful little pause in our Lenten days to celebrate the Solemnity of the Annunciation. This morning, in honor of the day, I have gone outside with my garden clippers and stepping lightly atop the crusty snow, snipped an armful of forsythia branches. They are a dull, grey brown with only a hint of tiny buds on the tips. I place them in vases full of water and wait. In a week or so, they should start responding to the warmth. First, the buds will swell, then some yellow will be visible on the very tips. Perhaps, by Easter they will be in full bloom.

The whole process can be an image of those months of waiting, after the exalted moment when Christ, Son of the Father, entered the womb of Mary. To all outward appearances, nothing had happened. But the God-Man was growing in her womb like the swelling buds.

First, came Mary's encounter with the Will of God as expressed by the angel. Her whole life had always been a sublime desire to know the will of God and then to act upon it. In an instant the angel places her into a new reality, revealing *The Plan* God has had in mind for an eternity. Mary has all the freedom to accept or reject. Yet, in a heartbeat, as soon as she knows the Divine Will, she gives her "Fiat."

What a sweet and enduring lesson for all of us. Mary is so tuned to God's frequency, that to begin with, she has no trouble recognizing Gabriel as the Divine messenger and then complying with that lovely assent that has been so oft-repeated through the ages: "Behold the handmaid of the Lord."

It is a fitting day to ponder my own vocation. Very often God uses a messenger for us, too, in order to help us know His will. For me, it was my friend, Lee.

After Tim's death, when the fog began to lift a bit and the grandchildren had all gone back home to Alabama, I was able to spend more time with a group of homeschooling friends from our parish. I saw Lee often at Mass and began helping her with the little bookstore and lending library in the vestibule of the church. After many months of discussion, I began to treasure this "holy friendship" and to see that God was filling that emptiness in my life with an idea.

It began with an invitation, "Would you like to come with us to our Carmelite meeting?" A door opened that I hadn't seen before.

As I walked through and looked around, I saw that it was good; it filled my life with a purpose. The idea came into sharper focus as I looked at it from all sides and zoomed in to inspect it further. Then came the most important part of the inspection—to shine the light of God upon it to see if this "fit" me. I must ask in prayer if this was God's will.

There's a lot more work for *us* than there was for Mary in discerning a vocation. She had God's word through the voice of an angel. We ordinary folk often stumble about for months or years, trying to listen better; to "translate" the events of our lives into the promptings that God is trying to whisper.

Happily, we in the Secular Carmelites, as in any vocation to the religious life, have a period of aspirancy so we can try on the "new clothes" and see if they fit.

A month from today, on April 25, I will have the chance to make my final promises as a member of the Secular Order of Discalced Carmelites. With my candle lit, I will proclaim my desire for my own sanctification and for the good of the Church to make this step. I will be asked if I wish to bind myself *"more strictly to the Church, in order to collaborate in her mission by means of contemplative prayer and apostolic activity."*

> Every Christian receives a vocation from God, a mission to fulfill, by means of which he is called to participate in the redemptive work of Jesus. For souls consecrated to God, this mission always finds its culminating point in a task of spiritual paternity or maternity. Oh, if every soul would respond to the divine appeal by as complete an acceptance as Mary's "Ecce ancilla Domini ... Fiat!" Behold the handmaid of the Lord ... Be it done! (Fr. Gabriel of St. Mary Magdalen, OCD, *Divine Intimacy*)

Yes!

Diary of a Country Carmelite

March 28, 2015

Though today is another cold and gray, wintry-feeling day, there is an air of warmth and celebration about despite the snow flurries. Our Carmelite community has the grace to be able to come together for a Day of Recollection. We drive to the welcoming arms of the church and put aside our usual activities and burdens for a morning and afternoon of prayer.

There are just 11 of us today, but when chanting Lauds and singing during the Mass, the 11 of us sound like a well-tuned choir and our voices fill the space with a joyful sound.

Today is the 500th anniversary of the birth of St. Teresa of Avila—and though it is Lent and we are about to begin Holy Week—there is another pause as we honor our Holy Mother and celebrate the gift that her life brings to our Order and to the whole Church.

For five years, Carmelite priests, nuns and layfolk have all been reading the works of Teresa together in a particular order. We have gone over her life, the foundations of her monasteries, her treatises on prayer and her letters. What a treasure chest this Doctor of the Church has left for us to open and explore!

Her personality beams from the pages of her writings; sometimes with humor, often digressing. We see her supreme love of God, her indomitable sense of mission, her courage and dedication to her "family". She has bequeathed us a timeless testament in her synthesis on prayer and in her description of the soul who is bathed in the light of God's love.

Today we pray together the six Sorrowful Mysteries of the Carmelite Rosary—adding a meditation on Mary receiving the body of her Son into her arms as he is taken down from the cross. Before each decade of the rosary we hear Teresa's words as she reflects upon the suffering Christ in the garden, in the tortuous drama of His scourging and in the laborious plodding up the hill to Calvary.

> The scene of His prayer in the garden, especially, was a comfort to me; I strove to be His companion there. I thought of the sweat and agony He had undergone in that place ... I remained with Him as long as my thoughts allowed me to.
>
> If I had understood as I do now that in this little palace of my soul dwelt so great a King, I would not have left Him alone so often. (Teresa of Jesus, *The Book of Her Life*)

We kept Jesus company along with Teresa, and it gave us all a sweet peace and sense of timelessness. Our prayers and comfort work outside of time to console the dear heart of Our Lord.

Our small group is one of a host of others celebrating today. In preparation, icons have been written, songs composed (*and* sung with a virtual choir on the internet!), scholars assembled to study her writings. One creative group solicited "selfies" of people holding images of St. Teresa and used them to spell out her name. Even her walking stick has been making a world tour.

Pope Francis imparted his Apostolic Blessing to the "Teresian Family" and penned a letter to our Superior General, Fr. Saverio Cannistra, including these thoughts:

> Saint Teresa is above all a teacher of prayer. Central in her experience of prayer was the discovery of the humanity of Christ. Moved by the desire to share this personal experience with others, she describes it in a vivid and simple way, available to all, because it consists simply in a "relation of friendship ... with Him who we know loves us". (*Life*, 8, 5) Many times her account itself is transformed into prayer, as if she wished to introduce the reader into her interior dialogue with Christ. Teresa's was not a prayer reserved only to a place or moment

of the day; it flowed spontaneously in the most diverse occasions: "It would be arduous if prayer could only be done in separated places." (*Foundations*, 5, 16) She was convinced of the value of continuous prayer, although not always perfect. The saint asks us to be perseverant, faithful even in the midst of aridity, personal difficulties or the pressing needs that call us. (Pope Francis, letter, March 28, 2015)

St. Teresa, herself, gives us her own encouragement:

Remember how St. Augustine tells us about his seeking God in many places and eventually finding Him within himself. Do you suppose it is of little importance that a soul which is often distracted should come to understand this truth and to find that, in order to speak to its Eternal Father and to take its delight in Him, it has no need to go to Heaven ... We need no wings to go in search of Him but only to find a place where we can be alone and look upon Him present within us. (*The Way of Perfection*, 28)

April

April 1, 2015

Holy Week has begun and I go about my day with quiet and determination, cleaning and planning for the days ahead. Dinner will be
a simple chicken soup, so I chop some vegetables and add them to
the carcass in the soup pot along with some herbs. As the fragrance
wafts through the house, I dust and straighten, then pull out my missal and breviary, so I won't forget them when I leave for noon Mass.

Today we commemorate St. Nuno Alvares Pereira, who first saw
the light of day in the middle of the 14th century in Portugal. Raised
in a castle in Ourem, near Fatima, Nuno grew up reading books about
knights and chivalry. When he was 13, he was taken to the court of
Fernando, King of Portugal, where his mother was the nurse and
companion to the royal princess, Beatriz. It was a time of great up-
heaval in Portugal, a devastating plague had just run out its course
and an equally horrific invasion, both military and religious in nature,
was commencing. The Castilian army in Spain was making inroads
into Portugal, often aided by the Portuguese nobility.

Knighted shortly after his arrival at court, Nuno was clearly disturbed as he watched King Fernando's inability to raise an army to
defend the country. It was not quite his time to fight, though. He
bowed to his father's wishes that he marry, and at 16 went to live on
the family's ancestral lands far away from the intrigues of the nobility.

Diary of a Country Carmelite

After ten years, his wife had died as had his two sons, leaving Nuno with a daughter, Beatriz, whom he loved greatly. His time on the estate had also given him a glimpse into the trials of the peasant folk with crop failures, marauding invaders and sickness beating them down. Where were the knights of chivalry when they were most needed to aid the poor and redress their wrongs?

It seems that Nuno felt himself being called out of his ordinary life and into the battle for his people and his country. He donned a suit of armor and, ever the faithful Catholic, had a standard made bearing images of the crucified Christ, the Madonna and Saints John, James and George. He confronted the royals who had made an alliance with the schismatic Castilians and raised an army among the people. For the next 17 years he lived the life of a soldier, but a very devout one, praying and fasting, receiving mystic revelations and in periodic times of calm, walking barefoot on pilgrimage to Marian shrines.

Battle by battle, and region by region his army was successful. In one of the most famous confrontations his band of 7000 men defeated 20,000 Castilians at Aljubarrota, rightly earning him the title "Constable of the Realm" in 1385.

His mission accomplished, Nuno hung up his sword and shield, made sure his daughter Beatriz was safe with her grandmother and set about divesting himself of his property. He gave his lands to his soldiers and tenants, grain to the needy, pardoned his debtors, despite the jealous complaints from other nobles, and then proceeded to build churches and a famous cathedral in Lisbon as well as founding a Carmelite monastery there.

Next began the third and final phase of our brave knight's life. In 1423, he entered the Carmelite monastery he had built, taking the name Nuno de Santa Maria, renouncing all his titles and accomplishments and walking the streets begging alms for the poor and feeding them soup when they came to the monastery. He died a simple and humble lay brother in 1431, the same year that a treaty was signed between Portugal and Castile, no doubt sped along by Nuno's prayers and sufferings for his beloved Portugal.

What a family we have yet to meet: men and women from all countries, economic stations and walks of life. United in the love of Christ and each bringing their virtues and works as the fruits of their labor, we see them side by side, beckoning us on to bravery and perseverance.

St. Nuno, pray for us and encourage us to never give up the fight, hang up our sword and shield ... or soup ladle and broom ... until God bids us to the blessed rest of those who have followed Him unreservedly.

> St Nuno allowed no obstacle to come in the way of God's action in his life, imitating Our Lady, to whom he was deeply devoted and to whom he publicly attributed his victories.
>
> ... I am glad to point this exemplary figure out to the whole Church particularly because he exercised his life of faith and prayer in contexts apparently unfavourable to it, as proof that in any situation, even military or in war time, it is possible to act and to put into practice the values and principles of Christian life, especially if they are placed at the service of the common good and the glory of God. (Pope Benedict, *Papal Homily, Canonization of St. Nuno*, April 26, 2009)

April 6, 2015

As if to echo the joy of Easter, our little corner of creation is singing today. There seems to be some gathering of twigs for nest building, just as our winter weariness fades with the melting snow. Alleluia!

Another Holy Week has been celebrated in all parts of the Christian world. In our corner, we pulled out our own family traditions—lamb stew and rosemary buns— on Thursday before the divine liturgy bursting with symbolism and beauty in the evening. A stark and quiet Good Friday was endured with our souls united in consoling Jesus. A Saturday of preparation next, then, bundled up against the cold, the blazing Easter Vigil fire ushering us once more into light and life and joy. With our candles lit we found our own spots back in the dark church—each of us little flames of hope in a dark world.

The forsythia branches that I brought inside on the Annunciation all burst into bloom on cue and I surrounded them on Easter morning with lilies and hyacinth, daffodils and tulips.

Meanwhile, Fr. Tom spent Holy Week and Easter in Mexico hearing confessions and offering Mass in a succession of little towns and villages. What a joy for us to unite ourselves with him and his Mass as we sit with Paul and the girls in their Easter best and Nicholas intent upon his duties at the altar.

In the afternoon before the grandchildren read the clues to find their Easter treats, Isabella remembers where we "buried" the Alleluia and runs to put it into place in front of the flowers and candles. We feast together with the family around the table, happily remembering those who feast in other places and our dear ones "who have gone before us marked with the sign of faith."

Joy in truth: According to the vibrant admonition of St. Paul, "Let us celebrate the feast, not with the old leaven ... but with the unleavened bread of sincerity and truth." In this world there are many ephemeral joys based on fragile, insecure foundations; but the Paschal joy is solidly grounded on the knowledge that we are in the truth, the truth which Christ brought to the world and which He confirmed by His Resurrection. The Resurrection tells us that our faith is not in vain, that our hope is not founded on a dead man, but on a living one, the Living One par excellence, whose life is so strong that it vivifies, in time

and in eternity, all those who believe in Him. (Fr. Gabriel of
St. Mary Magdalen, OCD, *Divine Intimacy*, 140.1)

April 13, 2015

The big pile of snow next to the house has almost melted and if I look
closely, I can see the daffodil spears just poking up through the dark
earth. I hung a load of clothes out on the clothesline this morning
and reveled in this simple, domestic chore. When I finished, I raked
up the tiny pinecones and needles in the front yard, soaking up the
sun and basking in the palpable feeling of contentment in working
outside once again.

Last week we had several wintry-like days and an ice storm. It
looked as if we were digressing and retreating back into those dark,
foggy winter days. Thankfully, another warm front moved in, and much
to our delight, the ice fell in little pieces from around the encrusted
branches; the woods and yard alive with the welcome clatter.

The change in weather also meant that our drive to the annual
Carmelite district retreat would be a safe one if we could just patiently
navigate the rush hour traffic on Friday afternoon. Three of us drove
together, meeting other secular Carmelites from around Boston, Rhode
Island and places north and west.

I was happy at the timing of the retreat, just two short weeks
away from my final profession. I brought along a meditation on the
Promise, hoping that I would be able to use my time apart to ponder
more deeply the meaning of the promises I would be making.

Sandwiched in between the liturgies and conferences on prayer
and the praying of the Liturgy of the Hours, I managed to read
and meditate on the various elements that would mark this step
in my life.

Diary of a Country Carmelite

I will be promising to *"tend toward evangelical perfection in the spirit of the evangelical counsels of chastity, poverty, obedience and of the Beatitudes … for the rest of my life"*, so I had *surely* better know what this means and how such a thing can be accomplished. I found a beautiful series of talks by the formation Director of a secular Community in St. Louis and printed them out to study and to "meditate in the heart".

This meditating, in imitation of Mary, who "pondered all these things in her heart", is at the core and center of life for a Carmelite. At the end of our promise, we entrust all to Mary and hold her up to be our model in prayer, in recollection during all the many and sundry activities of each day, in the blessed poverty she embraced, the obedience of her faithful spirit and the chaste and modest demeanor of her whole being.

Of course, unlike Mary, we carry the burden of sin, so ours can never be a perfect imitation, but we promise to always be "tending" toward that perfection.

Through adherence to the life the Beatitudes hold out to us, we live out the path that Christ holds out to all: the humility, detachment, meekness, mercy, thirst for God, purity, transformation through suffering and integrity of heart which dispose us to union with God.

Seen altogether it seems daunting and there is always the possibility that I will fail. Despite my littleness, though, there is ever and always God's grace which raises up our simple, humble attempts to progressively greater heights, for our promise is "inspired by the Holy Spirit, in response to God's call".

I met a group of women and men, from all walks of life; young and old and of many nationalities, all trying, with this grace, to live out the life of a Secular Carmelite. What a great example for me to see this fidelity to grace in action and to know that as part of the Carmelite family we hold one another up with our prayers and make this fidelity possible with our sacrifices, detachment and acceptance of God's will.

We ended our retreat on the Feast of Divine Mercy, which is the key to everything. With God's mercy and love, even the seemingly impossible is accomplished. What a marvel that we can be recipients of such a grace!

> Jesus needs nothing but your humility and your confidence to work marvels of purification and sanctification in you. And your confidence will be in proportion to your humility, because it is to the extent that we realize our need of Jesus that we have recourse to Him, and we sense this need to the extent that we justly realize our unworthiness. (Jean C.J. d'Elbée, *I Believe in Love*)

April 17, 2015

Spring is indeed taking a firm hold on the landscape. Green grass and clumps of spring bulbs in front gardens greet three of us as we drive west over hilly farmland to a small-town wake. Traveling along, Lee, Barb and I pray the Office of the Dead together for the father of another Carmelite and beg that his soul will speedily rest in God's embrace. We are a family joined together in a common purpose and want to eagerly go to meet Pete and his wife, Judith as they mourn Pete's father, Peter.

> Dear friends, how beautiful and consoling is the communion of saints! It is a reality that infuses a different dimension to our whole life. We are never alone! We form part of a spiritual "company" in which profound solidarity reigns: the good of each one is for the benefit of all and, vice versa, the common happiness is radiated in each one. It is a mystery that, in a certain measure, we can already experience in this world, in the family, in friendship, especially in the spiritual community

of the Church. May Mary Most Holy help us to walk swiftly on the way of sanctity and show herself a Mother of mercy for the souls of the deceased. (Pope Benedict XVI, Angelus Address, November 2, 2009)

Today we also think about a particular, saintly member of our Carmelite family, Blessed Baptist Spagnoli, on his feast day. He lived in Italy at the close of the 15th and beginning of the 16th century, and like Saints Peter Thomas and Andrew Corsini, had a prominent role to play in yet another turbulent era. Born in Mantua, Italy in 1447, Baptist Spagnoli made his Carmelite profession at the age of 17 and then went on for further studies in Bologna, earning a Master of Theology degree. It seems that his talents for leadership were recognized early on as he served as prior at Parma, five terms as Vicar General and one as Prior General of the Carmelite Order. Spagnoli also participated in the Fifth Lateran Council and was given diplomatic assignments like his confreres a century earlier.

All this would be enough to distinguish our Blessed Baptist in the eyes of history, but what he is most remembered for are the writings he left behind. He was an "uncommon literary genius" and a poet of illustrious renown. (Some studious Latin scholar could be of great help to us if they were to translate his voluminous collection of poetry!) He wrote poems in honor of popes, the Virgin Mary and about the pressing problems swirling around the turmoil of 15th- and 16th-century Italy. His poems were widely published in his day and he was often quoted, most famously by Shakespeare in *Love's Labor Lost*.

As Martin Luther would do a few decades later, he recognized the issues and abuses in the Church and the clergy and fought for reform, even addressing Pope Innocent VIII and the Cardinals in the Vatican Basilica in 1489. Unlike Luther, though, he wanted to maintain the authority of the Papacy and preserve the doctrine of the Church.

Spagnoli died in 1516 and the testimony of his sanctity—his incorrupt body—lies at rest in the cathedral in Mantua.

What does he have to say to us today in our world and in the Church where so much is different but also "nihil sub solum est novum?" Love for Christ and His Church, respect for the Pope, faithfulness, a dedication to Our Lady and always the desire to "speak the truth in love."

May God preserve the Church in every era and may our prayers, united to those of Christ and our fellow Carmelites the world over, serve as the spark for those preachers and apologists who serve as the voice of God.

April 18, 2015

Today is Saturday and Andy's 65th birthday. It is also the perfect day for the opening of the Little League season. The two of us head to Mass and enjoy a quick breakfast before splitting up for the morning. Andy has a regional planning meeting and I need to make a run to the grocery store for pie-making provisions.

Later, back at home, I peel, quarter and slice apples, roll out the dough and slide the full pies into the oven. It is contemplative work, steady and rhythmic, and I have the time to ponder a Carmelite whose life brings me great inspiration.

It is the feast day of Blessed Mary of the Incarnation, who began life in 16th-century Paris as Barbe Avrillot. She bowed to her mother's wish that she marry, and at 16, wed Pierre Acarie, becoming a capable housewife and mother of three sons and three daughters. Though moving in the heady circles of the Parisian nobility, Barbe possessed a firm faith, a humble common sense and was dedicated to the perfect fulfillment of her duties. She was an engaged mother, always seeking the best for her children with equal measures of humor and serious instruction.

Her mothering didn't end with her children, though. A steady stream of the destitute made their way to her back door and were not disappointed with her generous alms. Barbe also had the reputation for distributing inspired advice and her front door was busy as well with those who were uncertain and needed her counsel.

Life was not all ease and wealth either, in the Acarie household. Her husband, Pierre, made some disastrous decisions and was forced into exile. Barbe herself fell several times and suffered three leg fractures. Then at age 27, she was the recipient of an invisible stigmata, enduring the pain of the wounds of Christ's crucifixion.

Barbe fueled her spiritual life with reading, particularly the writings of St. Teresa of Avila, and was visited twice by the Virgin Mary, who instructed her "in the name of God" to bring the Carmelite Order to France.

When Mary speaks, her true daughters listen and act. Barbe sent delegates to Spain to bring the sisters to France where they arrived in 1604. After Pierre died in 1615, Barbe was professed as a lay sister in the Carmel of Amiens. Her three daughters also followed her into Carmel.

She was greatly esteemed by St. Francis de Sales, who held her up for her spirit of prayer and zeal for souls and the propagation of the faith, though it wasn't until 1781 that she was beatified.

What a lot to ponder in the life of this French gentlewoman. I think about the differences in the circumstances of our two lives as I slice apples and roll out dough. I have no servants or wealth to administer, no stigmata or direct line to Mary's voice, but I do try to imitate her strong habits of prayer and the concern for each soul who comes my way.

Later in the day, I sat and watched our granddaughter, Bella, debut as catcher, entertained Kateri and walked the dog as Andy cheered on

Nicholas at another ballfield several miles away. After the last players exited the field and we loaded everyone up into our cars we made our way up the hills to Blandford. Paul fired up the grill and cooked hamburgers in honor of his father's birthday and we feasted on the long-awaited apple pies.

Each day has its work and duties, family obligations and moments of joy. When lived with an eye on the eternal and with hearts immersed in prayer, every one of those days can become that offering to God the Father in union with Christ's own offering. Whether our work and prayer are carried out in 16th-century France or in 21st-century America, no matter. They still have the same value and the same worth.

> Some time later, as I happened to glance (with my bodily eyes) at a crucifix, my heart was touched so suddenly and vividly that I could no longer see it exteriorly but only interiorly. I was astonished to see the Second Person of the Most Holy Trinity placed in this position for my sins and for the sins of mankind. It would be quite impossible for me to explain what I felt interiorly, and to describe the excellence and dignity of that Second Person. The sight of this was so clear and had such an effect on me that I could not admit, let alone understand, how, with so many other ways of redeeming the world at His disposal; He had willed to demean something that was so worthy and so precious; then at length it pleased this same Lord to relieve my anguish (and I believe that if it had continued, I would have been unable to bear it), instructing me so specifically and effectively, and above all with so much clarity, that I could in no way doubt that it was He who bestowed light on my darkness and taught me, as a good father would teach his child, or a good master his disciple what I felt interiorly cannot be described, and even less put into words. I recall that my soul was in wonder at His wisdom, His goodness, and above all, the

excess of His love for mankind. Joy and suffering combined to produce divers effects and to bring a wealth of considerations to mind. (Blessed Mary of the Incarnation)

April 23, 2015

For several days this week I have been without a car, as the poor beast is in the shop for repairs. In some ways being homebound is not a problem for me. There is always plenty to do and it seems to add a greater sense of calm and quiet to my day. However, it also means missing Mass and that is a great loss for me. God's will is best recognized in what the circumstances of each day dictate, so there must be no worries or upset emotions.

Today, however, the car is ready! Andy drops me off at the repair shop on his way to work so that I can pay the bill and pick up the car. I drive to morning Mass, happy that I can once again participate in the great Sacrifice of Love and receive my Lord Jesus in Holy Communion.

Fortified for what lies ahead, I drive back up the hills for another day of work at Porter Memorial Library, Blandford's small center of literature, culture and information. As I work and greet neighbors who stop in, I keep in mind today's Carmelite, Blessed Teresa of the Cross Manetti. She was born in Florence in 1846 and given the name Teresa Adelaida Cesina Manetti. As a little girl she experienced her first loss with the death of her father, which perhaps opened her heart to the plight of those without parents.

Gathering around her other young women, Teresa and her friends lived a common life as they prayed, worked and read together. In 1874 they formed a Teresian Third Order with our young Carmelite taking the name Teresa Mary of the Cross. Several years later the women began offering shelter to orphans and in short order there was a need for a larger house. In 1888 they started wearing the Carmelite habit and after a name change came to be known as the Third Order Carmelite Sisters of St. Teresa.

Sr. Teresa Mary's work multiplied as others joined her over time. Now there were twelve orphanages in Tuscany, two in Syria and one in Haifa on the slopes of Mount Carmel. She felt herself to be a servant of the orphans and sought always to be available to them and also to those in the community. Crowds of people came to speak to her, no doubt recognizing Christ radiating from her being. All left consoled and strengthened for their own sufferings.

Teresa had a great sense of recollection and felt herself to be united with God at every moment, but most especially at the reception of Holy Communion, where she often remained in ecstasy.

No doubt this great devotion was behind her desire to found a house of Perpetual Adoration. Desire became action and she built a house in Florence for this very purpose.

She was Teresa Mary *of the Cross* by name and chose, too, the path of suffering. It was granted to her physically in the form of a painful cancer in her later years and spiritually in a palpable "dark night" of deprivation. She died in 1910 and was beatified in 1986 by Pope St. John Paul II. She is the patron of those ridiculed for their piety.

I pause at my work at the computer and think again of how God orders our days so well when we place ourselves at His service, bringing people into our orbit and permitting circumstances which we can turn to good. It is not always easy, but as Teresa Mary said,

God makes saints with a chisel, not a paintbrush.

Suddenly the dark skies and snow pellets of this grey April day fade away as my two granddaughters walk into the library with their mother and I open my arms for hugs. While Mom picks out a stack of books for them, I put on the tea kettle and bring out the animal crackers, happy for a little diversion and thanking God, with Teresa

Mary, for that chisel in the hand of God and also for the soft brush that sweeps away the chips of stone dust.

April 25, 2015
Profession Day

At last the long-awaited day has arrived. I make sure that I haven't forgotten anything and stow my bags in the back of Lee's car for the hour drive north to Turners Falls. We arrive early, schlepping our loads of food, flowers and books down to the undercroft to await our celebration.

I make my excuses after a bit and head upstairs to church, hoping for a few minutes of quiet in order to compose myself before the Blessed Sacrament, determined as I am to have this day proceed with a calm and peaceful spirit.

Soon the others in our community join me and we begin by chanting Morning Prayer together. Today is the Feast of St. Mark, the Evangelist, so we have the Propers of the day and the psalms set aside for feasts.

> For your love is better than life,
> My lips will speak your praise.
> So I will bless you all my life,
> in your name I will lift up my hands,
> My soul shall be filled as with a banquet,
> my mouth shall praise you with joy.
> (Psalm 63:4-6)

Already we begin the praise of joy and it continues when Mass begins and proceeds through all the particular ceremonies set aside for this day. So much is made meaningful through the readings and psalms of the Mass. For Lynda, who is just receiving her scapular we hear the First Reading from St. Peter, *"Beloved: Clothe yourselves with humility …"* They are very good words to ponder as the squares of brown cloth are placed over her shoulders. Next was Debbie, now also known as Deborah Mary of the Divine Mercy, come to pronounce her Temporary Profession. Perhaps she was echoing the Responsorial Psalm … *"For ever I will sing the goodness of the Lord"*, when instead of promising *"for three years"*, she said *"for the rest of my life"*. We all smile at her enthusiasm.

Next, I take my place in front of the altar rail with Peter and Judith. With our blessed candles lit, Fr. Chris gives each of us a turn to make our solemn promise before God and all the witnesses assembled. When it is my turn I speak my profession with determination and joy.

> I, Ana Thérèse of the Eucharistic Heart of Jesus, inspired by the Holy Spirit, in response to God's call, sincerely promise to the Superior of the Order of the Teresian Carmel, and to you, my brothers and sisters, to tend toward evangelical perfection in the spirit of the evangelical counsels of chastity, poverty, obedience and of the Beatitudes, according to the Rule of St. Albert and the Constitutions of the Secular Order of the Discalced Carmelites for the rest of my life.
>
> I confidently entrust this, my Promise, to the Virgin Mary, Mother and Queen of Carmel.

Our intentions and promises are all sealed with the reception of Holy Communion and those sweet minutes of our thanksgiving conversations with Our Lord.

And later with humble thanks to Mary as we sing, "Regina Coeli, Laetare, Alleluia."

Before leaving church we mark the day with photographs then turn to greet our family and friends who came along to be with us for this momentous day. There are my mother and father here from

Diary of a Country Carmelite

New York, Andy with his camera, our son Paul and his wife, Jasmine, with their three children, my brother, Steve and sister-in-law, Gail from Connecticut and my niece, Monica, who braved a train ride from Virginia.

I am surprised to see that my brother-in-law, Jim the photographer, is there as well, and my friend, Mary Ann, who has taken time out from her farm chores and her own birthday celebration to come today. How blessed I am in my family and friends!

We head down to the undercroft for a banquet and visits with our Carmelite brothers and sisters and all who have joined us. Oh, happy day!

Later that night before heading to bed, I replayed the day's events and with a heart full to the brim offered a thanksgiving to God for *everything*. For Fr. Thomas in Rome who sent photographs of his early morning trek to one of the Carmelite churches in Rome, Santa Maria della Scala in Trastevere, where he offered Mass for me, remarking on the fittingness of Saturday's eve of Good Shepherd Sunday and the 52nd World Day of Prayer for Vocations. For those who celebrated with me and those who could not but sent along their love and prayers. For the happy household who cooked and feasted with us at home afterwards. For my 9-year-old granddaughter, Isabella, who finally asks, "Grandma, exactly what is a Carmelite?" For the end of the day, chanting Evening Prayer on the porch before everyone heads home. For the gift of my vocation.

I proclaim a solemn *Te Deum* and joyful *Alleluia*!

> You are God, we praise you:
> You are the Lord: we acclaim you;
> You are the eternal Father:
> All creation worships you.
> To you all angels, all the powers of heaven,
> Cherubim and Seraphim, sing in endless praise:

Holy, holy, holy, Lord God of power and might,
Heaven and earth are full of your glory.
The glorious company of apostles praise you.
The noble fellowship of prophets praise you.
The white-robed army of martyrs praise you.
Throughout the world, the holy Church acclaims you:
Father of majesty unbounded,
Your true and only Son, worthy of all worship,
And the Holy Spirit, advocate and guide.
You, Christ, are the King of Glory
The eternal Son of the Father.
When you became man to set us free,
You did not spurn the Virgin's womb.
You overcame the sting of death,
And opened the kingdom of heaven to all believers.
You are seated at God's right hand in glory.
We believe that you will come and be our judge.
Come then, Lord, and help your people,
Bought with the price of your own blood,
And bring us with your saints to glory everlasting.

Charity gave me the key to my vocation. I understood that if
the Church has a body composed of different members, the
noblest and most necessary of all the members would not
be lacking to her. I understood that the Church has a heart,
and that this heart burns with Love. I understood that Love
alone makes its members act, that if this Love were to be extinguished, the Apostles would no longer preach the Gospel,
the Martyrs would refuse to shed their blood.... I understood
that Love embraces all vocations, that Love is all things, that it
embraces all times and all places ... in a word, that it is eternal!
(St. Thérèse of Lisieux)

May

May 1, 2015

Yesterday we Carmelites fasted in preparation for today's feast of St. Joseph the Worker, so today, we pause and celebrate. Joseph has the illustrious title of *Protector of Carmel*, so it is fitting that we have this second day in the liturgical year in his honor in order to consider, in closer detail, his model as industrious worker. The two ideas dovetail nicely, as one of the primary ways that a father protects his family is through his faithful and constant labor.

The Church has always taught that any honest work has dignity and that this work can be the means for our sanctification. Work done well, with attention to detail, and then, completed faithfully, always fits the bill. It is no matter that this work is humble, (I remember when our boys were little and all wanted to be garbage men), or of a loftier sort.

In the Church, each one of us has his mission to fulfill for the good of souls and the glory of God. This mission requires work—often fatiguing work—and much sacrifice and intense activity. Like St. Joseph, we must give ourselves generously and totally, without sparing, without reserve, but, at the same time, we must also give ourselves to the works of God with a heart filled with God, with a heart which lives with Him in an intimacy nourished by the assiduous exercise of prayer. St.

Diary of a Country Carmelite

Joseph teaches us the blessed secret of a life of combined activity and contemplation, so that, following his example, we may give ourselves to the active life without neglecting our life of intimate union with God. (Fr. Gabriel of St. Mary Magdalen, OCD, *Divine Intimacy*)

My work today is so gloriously varied. I feed the chickens and open up the coop so they can forage in the grass, I bake two loaves of bread, frame some icons that are destined as gifts, tidy up the kitchen and start some laundry.

The most perfect work, even when it is a steady labor, is best performed in the silent prayer of recollection, praising God for the glory of a spring day as I walk to the barn; marveling at the aroma coming forth from the oven as the bread is baking and thanking God for the bounty in my pantry. Interceding for my fellow Carmelites as I position the icons in their frames, all the while thinking of Mary and Joseph as they went about their ordinary work.

The recollection becomes deeper as I pause and drive to Mass and more intimately consider St. Joseph and his great dignity. During Mass I am "working", too, in best Carmelite fashion, praising God and begging His help for those without jobs, for holy priests, for fathers of families and for each of us that we will come to know our dignity as workers in the great vineyard of souls.

More pondering on the quiet drive home, more laundry, more cooking and baking as I prepare the fish chowder and cornbread to serve Andy for dinner tonight. Then I "treat" myself to some of the work that I love best of all as I head out to the garden. I weed a little and find here, too, some fertile matter for meditation as I clear away the dry leaves and see the tightly-wound hosta spears poking through the soil, some miniature daffodils blooming and pulmonaria flowers standing up straight on their short stems. The visible results of my work, just as one day I will see what has come of my prayers.

Later in the evening, Andy and I sit down to pray a Rosary and continue in quiet the work of this day. With Joseph in mind we begin, too, a month dedicated to Mary. May all our heavenly host keep us strong for the task.

> The setting sun now dies away,
> And darkness comes at close of day;
> Your brightest beams, dear Lord impart,
> And let them shine within our heart.
>
> We praise your name with joy this night:
> Please watch and guide us till the light;
> Joining the music of the blest,
> O Lord, we sing ourselves to rest.
> (*Jam sol recedit igneus*)

May 8, 2015

The weather has been so summer-like for the past few weeks that the spring growth has gotten ahead of itself. All of a sudden, the suggestion of leaves on the maple and oak trees has burst into reality and the view across the road is now one mass of many shades of green. It is glorious and fills me with joy. Turning from the distance to the beauty close at hand, I kneel in front of the flower beds, weeding and trimming back last year's old growth. I take in the sight before me—daffodils, hyacinths and primrose in bloom, small roses leafing out, points of hosta leaves shooting up and bleeding heart leaves turning from red to green.

All winter we northerners have been starved for green and growth and now we are awash in it. What a lift for our spirits! It is a busy time of year, planning and planting our gardens, sharing perennials and meeting with the Garden Club to plan the spring gardens in the center of town.

"Carmel" means garden. I think of the original abundance in Eden; all beauty and fruitfulness and similarly, the life of grace we have been given in Christ. There must be a fountain in the garden or a stream to make the image complete for Christ is "the fount of all holiness."

Mary, Our Lady of Mount Carmel, is the enclosed garden—set aside and bordered by a hedge of green in my image—where she adores the Triune God, hidden inside.

I think Mary and our Tim have been walking in the eternal garden, conspiring today to bring joy to another mother. Over the years we had lost contact with Tim's birth mother when she moved away. I have been praying that one day we would find her again so I could fill in all the blanks in Tim's life and share with her his sweet personality and capacity for joy.

Thanks to the web of connectedness and an adept search engine, her daughter-in-law contacts me and we have our first phone conversation in 25 years. How amazing! What a joy for me to talk about Tim to the one who wants to hear most.

I wrap up the book of Tim's life and decide to slip in some extra photographs. They won't arrive in time for Mother's Day, but my prayers for her will and also my thanksgiving to Christ Jesus and His dear Mother for this sweet gift, so long withheld.

Deo Gratias!

May 14, 2015

I follow Andy's truck down the hills to our Ascension Thursday Mass this morning, enclosed in quiet. The silence and solitude are a good preparation for Mass but I do appreciate the fact that we can be together for this holy day before we each go our separate ways. Andy heads off to work while I stay behind to pray the Divine Office in the stillness of the church.

In honor of the day I make my way to a small favorite restaurant and get my cup of tea and egg sandwich, then spread out my papers and write in leisure for a while.

There is so much to ponder in the Mass readings for this day.

You will receive power when the Holy Spirit comes upon you, and you will be my witnesses in Jerusalem, throughout Judea and Samaria, and to the ends of the earth. (Acts 1:8)

May the eyes of your hearts be enlightened, that you may know what is the hope that belongs to this call, what are the riches of glory in his inheritance among the holy ones, and what is the surpassing greatness of his power for us who believe. (First Reading: Ephesians 1:18-19a)

We are urged to *"clap our hands"* and *"shout ... with cries of gladness"* today as we see in our mind's eye Christ ascending, literally and truly, to the Father in heaven. He goes to prepare a place for us and to send His parting gift—His Holy Spirit. How privileged we are to be the recipients of such a gift! Are we ever grateful enough?

St. Augustine, in the Office of Readings, says that our hearts should be ascending with Christ, but that we still have that call as members of His body on earth to be witnesses ... *"to the ends of the earth".*

Christ is now exalted above the heavens, but he still suffers on earth with all the pain that we, the members of his body, have to bear ...

Why do we not strive to find rest with him in heaven even now, through the faith, hope and love that unites us to him? While in heaven he is also with us; and we while on earth are with him. He is here with us by his divinity, his power and his love. We cannot be in heaven, as he is on earth, by divinity, but in him, we can be there by love. (St Augustine, Office of Readings: Second Reading, Ascension)

I hold onto these thoughts during my busy hours at the library and pull them out again in silence and in solitude later on as I kneel in the garden, "together in love", praying in thanksgiving for that great parting gift.

> O LORD JESUS CHRIST, Who before ascending into Heaven didst promise to send the Holy Ghost to finish Thy work in the souls of Thine Apostles and Disciples, deign to grant the same Holy Spirit to me, that He may perfect in my soul the work of Thy grace and Thy love.
> Grant me the Spirit of Wisdom, that I may despise the perishable things of this world and aspire only after the things that are eternal;
> the Spirit of Understanding, to enlighten my mind with the light of Thy Divine truth;
> the Spirit of Counsel, that I may ever choose the surest way of pleasing God and gaining Heaven;
> the Spirit of Fortitude, that I may bear my cross with Thee and that I may overcome with courage all the obstacles that oppose my salvation;
> the Spirit of Knowledge, that I may know God and know myself and grow perfect in the science of the Saints;
> the Spirit of Piety, that I may find the service of God sweet and amiable;
> the Spirit of Fear, that I may be filled with a loving reverence towards God and may dread in any way to displease Him.
> Mark me, Dear Lord, with the sign of Thy true disciples, and animate me in all things with Thy Spirit. Amen.
> (Prayer for the Seven Gifts of the Holy Spirit)

May 16, 2015

I begin my day as I begin all days, with a half hour of mental prayer followed by Morning Prayer from the Liturgy of the Hours. It is always and ever the perfect way to start a new day—placing myself in the Presence of God for that quiet thirty minutes and then joining with all my fellow Carmelites and Catholics around the globe as we offer up the same antiphons, psalms, readings, responses and intercessions on behalf of the Church and the world. Though I pray alone in my quiet house, my voice blends with countless others to praise God and to beg help for our suffering world.

After some meditative house cleaning, I head out to Mass, where again, alone in my solitary pew, I join with thousands of other solitaries in the penultimate prayer—alone and not alone.

Back at home I make my way out to the garden plots for an afternoon of soil preparation. Soon it will be time to plant seeds and baby seedlings, but if I don't weed, amend the soil, dig out some rocks and move a few invading strawberry and blackberry plants, I will have a poor crop this year.

I think of today's Carmelite, St. Simon Stock, as I dig and rake. Today happens to be the 750th anniversary of his death in Bordeaux in 1265. From various accounts he lived as a hermit in the English countryside near Kent, possibly living in a hollow oak tree if we can trust one historical account. In the early 13th century he joined the Carmelite order and after several decades was elected Prior General.

As with many visionary religious leaders, he was trying to adapt an ancient way of life to changing social conditions, so petitioned Pope Innocent IV to make some alterations in the Rule that would allow the friars to move into urban centers and university life. Simon was preparing the soil for new growth in a new age.

Diary of a Country Carmelite

Of course, we also know him as the saint who received the brown scapular from the hands of Our Lady, the vison having taken place in 1251. Ever devoted to Mary, he was handed her livery—two brown rectangles of cloth—to mark him and his friars as her particular servants, with the promise of their faithful service to be rewarded with her prompt gifts after death. Today, so many of us, friars, nuns, seculars and ordinary Catholics follow suit, wearing brown scapulars of various sizes and ornamentation, but all pledging our fealty as sons and daughters of Mary.

Just as men take pride in having others wear their livery, so the most Holy Mary is pleased when her servants wear Her Scapular as a mark that they have dedicated themselves to Her service, and are members of the family of the Mother of God. (St. Alphonsus)

There is a dark sea that we all have to cross, remote from this comfortable world of our experience, opening up new dangers, and wider horizons. Over that sea the calm eyes of our blessed Lady look out, foreseeing the difficulties of our passage. And it was to the order of Mount Carmel that she gave the holy scapular, to be a life-belt in that sea, a talisman amid those unseen perils. She is not content to be our Mother in this world; she will care for us and see us into the next. (Ronald Knox, Sermon at Our Lady of Mount Carmel and St. Simon Stock Church, London, Feast of Our Lady of Mount Carmel, 16 July 1937)

May 18, 2015

Today a slow-moving fellow in blue jeans and suspenders delivers a load of topsoil to our house—a Mother's Day present from Andy. I feel so honored! It isn't everyone who receives such a unique and well-appreciated gift. It will take us a while to shovel it into wheelbarrows and apportion it out as bounty to some weary vegetable and flower beds. We plan on having our grandson, Nicholas, give us a hand this week so it won't be such a chore for us old folks.

Yesterday Nick's sisters, Bella and Tiri, came up the hill with us after Mass, and since it was a Sunday, we actually had a chance to enjoy the yard and gardens. We ate lunch with the girls at the picnic table and later moved some chairs under the birch trees in the back to read in the shade.

Half a world away, Pope Francis canonized four remarkable nuns, one of whom was a Carmelite, Mariam Baouardy, now Saint Mary of Jesus Crucified.

Today I read the words of the Holy Father for the occasion:

The Apostles had a direct and overwhelming experience of the resurrection; they were eyewitnesses to that event. Thanks to their authoritative testimony, many people came to believe; from faith in the risen Lord, Christian communities were born and are born continually. We too, today, base our faith in the risen Lord on the witness of the Apostles, which has come down to us through the mission of the Church. Our faith is firmly linked to their testimony, as to an unbroken chain which spans the centuries, made up not only by the successors to the Apostles, but also by succeeding generations of Christians. Like the Apostles … each one of Christ's followers is called to become a witness to his resurrection, above all in those human settings where forgetfulness of God and human disorientation are most evident.

If this is to happen, we need to "remain in the risen Christ and in his love" as the First Letter of St. John has reminded us. "He who abides in love abides in God and God abides in him". This is the secret of the saints.

Diary of a Country Carmelite

From this eternal love between the Father and the Son, poured into our hearts from the Holy Spirit (cf. Romans 5:5), our mission and our fraternal communion draws strength; this love is the ever flowing source of our joy in following the Lord along the path of his poverty, his virginity and his obedience; and this same love calls us to cultivate contemplative prayer. Sister Mariam Baouardy experienced this in an outstanding way. Poor and uneducated, she was able to counsel others and provide theological explanations with extreme clarity, the fruit of her constant converse with the Holy Spirit.

What lofty words for such a humble little nun! And what marvels the Holy Spirit accomplished in her life.

Today, in this Seventh Week of Easter as we pray for the coming of the Holy Spirit in our lives, amidst the days of the novena preceding Pentecost, the Church has us ponder these thoughts in the Office of Readings. Oh, how everything fits together in God's marvelous way! St. Cyril of Jerusalem explains it in this manner:

His action is different in different people, but the Spirit himself is always the same. In each person, Scripture says, "the Spirit reveals his presence in a particular way for the common good".

The Spirit comes gently and makes himself known by his fragrance.

The strong fragrance of lilacs fills the air right now, reminding me of Tim's whisper after communion one day, "Mom, I taste something sweet. I think it is the Holy Spirit."

St. Cyril continues to explain how the Holy Spirit makes himself known:

He is not felt as a burden, for he is light, very light. Rays of light and knowledge stream before him as he approaches. The Spirit comes with the tenderness of a true friend and protector to save, to heal, to teach, to counsel, to strengthen, to console. The Spirit comes to enlighten the mind of the one who receives him, and then, through him, the minds of others as well. (*Catechetical Lectures* 16)

What marvels the Holy Spirit worked in the life of the "Little Arab"; orphaned, once left for dead, working as a maid, the Spirit eventually led her to Carmel where she was just such a one who healed, taught and enlightened. (See the August 25 entry to learn more about her.)

May 22, 2015

It is so easy this time of year for me to be overwhelmed. Besides all the daily household affairs to attend to, the library work, shopping, writing deadlines and volunteer commitments, there are the flower beds all quickly filling up with fast-growing and firmly-rooted weeds. I can't imagine how I will ever get caught up with this load of chores.

Of course, there is always a spiritual cure and I administer it daily and sometimes minute by minute. "Rest in the will of God," I remind myself, "for He doesn't expect the impossible." I follow this up with a quick prayer, "What are the next two things I should do?" It always works, but the cure must be repeated often!

When I pray the Office of Readings today I get more help from the Carmelite saint of the day, Joachina de Vedruna de Mas, who gives this advice in a letter:

We must not give in to weariness: we must spend every minute in loving God. God alone, the maker of heaven and earth, must be our rest and our consolation. The love of God is the only thing we can possess forever; everything else will pass away.

Diary of a Country Carmelite

I love this prescription of St. Joachina's and know that she must have dealt with an overloaded schedule herself.

She was born in Barcelona in 1783 and grew up in a time of turmoil in Spain. Drawn to the Carmelite Order from an early age, she was persuaded by her parents to marry, but thankfully, they chose a virtuous Catholic husband for her. Together they raised nine children. What household duties she must have had!

Her husband, Teodoro, gave up his career as a lawyer to fight in the Spanish army against the invasion of Napoleon, so leaving Joachina and the children to manage on their own. He resigned his position when the war ended but didn't live long afterward. Joachina was a widow at 33, but thanks to the family's wealth was able to concentrate on raising her children and caring for the sick. When all were settled in life, she returned to the desire of her youth and founded the Carmelites of Charity in 1826, where she used her talents in educating the young and tending the infirm.

Inspired by her example, many young women came to join in her endeavor. By the end of her life she had begun 19 communities to carry out the works of mercy that called to them. Persecutions and misunderstandings always seem to follow any good undertaking and our foundress, Joachina, was not exempt from them. During another period of war in Spain, she was accused, imprisoned and forced into exile, then later came under suspicion by her bishop. Valiantly she pressed on, making her active work all the more fruitful as it was supported and fed by her contemplative prayer.

> In spite of all that I am currently living, that I have already lived through, and all that I am seeing, God always sustains me by giving me courage so that I do not completely succumb. This is why, my daughter, I can affirm that on the way of the cross it is Jesus who carries it. Amen. Forward! (Joachina de Vedruna de Mas, letter)

What a lovely example for me to follow! No more weariness or wilting under the hot sun. Every moment spent in loving God, redirecting that will of mine that wants to quit or collapse in desperation, holding on to God alone! My weeds will only last for a season after all, but any work that I do with love in His name will flower and fruit in the eternal Garden.

May 25, 2015

Yesterday was Pentecost Sunday, a beautiful day to revel in Christ's gift to the Church. Today we honor Mary, under the title Mother of the Church. More beauty! We contemplate Mary, spouse of the Holy Spirit, present with the Apostles in the Upper Room at the first Pentecost and the great support and sustenance of the nascent Church. She still watches over that Church with a mother's love and guidance.

In an interesting convergence of celebrations this year, today we also commemorate St. Mary Magdalene de Pazzi, a Carmelite of the 16th century. Born in Florence as Catherine de Pazzi, she was attracted to prayer even as a young girl. Entering the Carmelite convent in Florence, she became known for her mystical ecstasies, especially after the reception of Communion. St. Mary Magdalene de Pazzi also endured a long period of spiritual dryness and severe temptations.

She was commissioned by Christ, during her ecstasies, to work for the reform of the Church and a renewal of religious life—a theme which fits very well with today's observance of Mary, Mother of the Church.

Despite these lofty gifts, our little Carmelite sister was a model religious, performing duties in the kitchen or laundry with perfection and particularly eager to serve the sick and elderly sisters. She died in 1607 and was canonized in 1669. Her body remains incorrupt to this day.

In this excerpt from her writings we get a sense of the mystical unity with the Trinity she enjoyed and the Holy Spirit's role in that unity.

> Come, Holy Spirit. Let the precious pearl of the Father and the Word's delight come. Spirit of truth, you are the reward of the saints, the comforter of souls, light in the darkness, riches to the poor, treasure to lovers, food for the hungry, comfort to those who are wandering; to sum up, you are the one in whom all treasures are contained.
>
> Come! As you descended upon Mary that the Word might become flesh, work in us through grace as you worked in her through nature and grace.
>
> Come! Food of every chaste thought, fountain of all mercy, sum of all purity.
>
> Come! Consume in us whatever prevents us from being consumed in you.

Coming down from the heights of Holy Mass and these sublime thoughts, I make my way back up the hills to our little town's Memorial Day celebration, complete with parade and picnic. Back at home, Andy and I spend our afternoon working outside. There is a slight breeze that keeps away the black flies so I am able to give my attention to the planting, mowing and weeding without the usual swatting of the pesky bugs. The peace also makes it easier to give rise to meditation as I work in the welcome sun, thanking God, along with St. Mary Magdalene de Pazzi for the *"precious pearl of the Father and the Word's delight"* and His *"work in us through grace."*

The day ends with a grey sky of clouds framing the back field and the borders of forest. I put away my tools and tidy up the barn, resting in that sweet peace and grateful for another day overflowing with grace.

May 29, 2015

Every so often a day comes up that affords something different … a break in the pattern of routine. Such a day can prove to be a sweet respite in a busy week.

After Mass this morning with two of my Carmelite friends, Lee and Lynda, I sat down for breakfast at a little diner. As Secular Carmelites we don't have the convent for community and solidarity, so we are grateful for the days when we can spend some time with one another, talk about what we are reading and dish out some encouragement as needed.

Later in the day, back at home I welcomed three women who came to piece a quilt for one of their daughters. It was another sweet break in the ordinary routine of life that gave rise to creativity and artistry. The making of something beautiful always brings me joy and provides another sort of respite that carries over into the more mundane work of each day.

Today's Carmelite, Blessed Elia (or Elisha) of St. Clement, knew how to ply her hand at the needle, so perhaps she, too, found a similar joy.

Theodora Fracasso was born in 1901 in Bari, Italy; one of nine children in a good Catholic family. She grew up under the direction of nuns and on several occasions had dreams that encouraged her in the spiritual life. On the night before her First Communion Theodora heard St. Thérèse of the Child Jesus tell her, "You will be a nun like me."

This was a few years off, however. First would come her school years, attendance at a workshop for sewing and embroidery and entrance into the Third Order Dominicans.

Diary of a Country Carmelite

Theodora exhibited a great desire to be of service to others as she grew older and had many opportunities during the war years in Italy to practice charity among her neighbors and to work as a catechist. Thanks to the insight of a wise spiritual director, she was guided towards the Carmelites and in 1920 was clothed as Sr. Elisha of St. Clement.

Sr. Elisha grew in virtue and holiness as she navigated life in her community. She was assigned to work on an embroidery machine at the girls' boarding school adjacent to the Carmel and then later worked at hand embroidery in her cell and as sacristan.

In 1927, a seemingly ordinary flu-like illness struck her and there followed almost a year of severe headaches. In her desire to bear up with courage she spoke no words of complaint. By the time she was diagnosed with possible meningitis or maybe encephalitis, it was too late to offer her any remedy.

Sr. Elisha had the great joy to die on Christmas Day in 1927. She was beatified by Pope Benedict XVI in 2006. In this excerpt from her writings, included in the Office of Readings for her memorial today, we get a little glimpse into the sweet soul of this simple nun.

My life is love: this sweet nectar surrounds me, this merciful love penetrates me, purifies me, renews me and I feel it consuming me. The cry of my heart is: "Love of my God, my soul searches for You alone. My soul, suffer and be quiet; love and hope; offer yourself but hide your suffering behind a smile, and always move on. I want to spend my life in deep silence, in the depths of my heart, in order to listen to the gentle voice of my sweet Jesus. Souls, I will find a way to cast you into the sea of Merciful Love: souls of sinners, but above all souls of priests and religious. To this end my existence is slowly disappearing, consumed like the oil of a lamp which watches near the Tabernacle."

I sense the vastness of my soul, its infinite greatness that the immensity of this world cannot contain: it was created to lose itself in You, my God, because you alone are great, infinite and thus You alone can make it completely happy.

Later in the day I have a chance to putter in the garden before it grows dark. I plant some herbs and tomatoes, pull a few weeds and collect the day's eggs, the quiet of the evening providing a soothing ending to a busy day. It also gives me the quiet and calm for reflection and I mull over these words of the little Italian Carmelite and make them my own, all the while attempting to imitate her deep silence so I, too, can hear that Voice of voices and find myself ready to *"lose itself in You, my God."* Really, the work of a lifetime, but with St. Elisha's help, hopefully, I will be one of the souls she will cast into the sea of Merciful Love.

June

June 7, 2015

I am writing in the green expanse of back lawn between the raspberry patch and a little circular garden with a dwarf Japanese red maple in its center. The breeze and the sun work together to make it one of those perfect days. And, as it is Sunday, I can relax and forget that there are weeds to conquer and plants to move.

Today is another joyous confluence of feasts and memorials. On the liturgical calendar, it is Corpus Christi Sunday and when June 7th does not fall on a Sunday, the memorial of Blessed Anne of St. Bartholomew. *And* on our family's calendar of remembrances, we mark the tenth anniversary of our son Tim's death.

I do *so* miss that boy! Ten years have sped by faster than I could have imagined. In the intervening years the wound has healed a bit and the scar faded somewhat. The absence of one so dearly loved is always felt, though, and especially so when the loss is experienced by a mother for a child.

Andy and I drove to the cemetery after Mass this morning and planted a red petunia in the little garden I have made round Tim's tombstone. What a comfort that he is buried in a little country cemetery where there are few rules about what can be planted around the grave markers. I can make it a sweet memorial garden with perennials brought from home and circled by small rocks. Andy poured water on all the plants and pulled a few weeds.

On the liturgical front, today's perfect gem of a feast serves to remind us of the great love God has for us. Not being content to enter our world and take on the humanity of a creature, to suffer horribly under torture and to die the excruciating death of crucifixion, Christ has chosen to remain with us, to be our consolation, our strength and our joy in this land of exile. We profess our belief today that in the hands of the priest and under the formula of consecration, the bread and wine are transformed into Christ. He truly lives on our altars and in our tabernacles, leaving us no longer orphans and no longer bereft of His help, His sustenance and His comfort. How blessed we are!

I know with a deep conviction that my mourning for Tim has been mitigated, soothed and sweetened (yes, sweetened is the right word) by my daily drive to Mass; my meeting with the best grief counselor under the sun; the sweetest Guest of my soul. I meet Tim in the Eucharistic presence of Christ, too, where I say to both Tim and Jesus: "I love you! I will always love you! Never stop! Famous words!" Tim's pre-hug ritual is mine now, too. Christ gives me the hug and brings Tim, too. "How can I keep from singing?"

Today the icing on the cake is my sweet Ana de San Bartolomé. In the year after Tim's death, when I was writing as the "country mother", I was also learning about Carmelite life and trying it on for size. It was then that I read about Ana and her life. The date of her feast day seemed to be a confirmation for me that this was the next step in my life ... the open door, the call to mission and purpose again.

Ana, or Anne for us English speaking folks, was born in Spain in 1549. Her parents were farmers, but particularly devout, Catholic farmers. Life was good for their little girl; the family went to Mass together every day and she developed a deep prayer life. Unlike most devout little girls, though, she often conversed with Christ and Our Lady. Jesus appeared to her often; usually He was just as tall as she, so they "grew" together. When she was ten, both of Anne's parents died in a plague. Her older brothers took over her care and they were not always gentle or understanding.

They didn't forget their parents' upbringing, though. When Anne became gravely ill they began a novena to St. Bartholomew and took her to the apostle's shrine and she was cured. Still, they pressured the little shepherdess to marry and made life difficult for her hoping she would give in. Once when she fell asleep while praying a rosary, she had a dream in which Mary showed her the Carmelite convent in Avila. To further make the point, she "saw" Jesus pulling her there by her rosary beads. (I can almost hear Tim laughing at that image!) When she was twenty-one, Anne mustered all her courage, left home and was professed as a lay sister by St. Teresa at St. Joseph's in Avila.

She worked as the convent's infirmarian and cared lovingly for Teresa when she broke her arm. Since Teresa was not able to write for a while she needed a secretary. Anne suited her but there was one problem. She could read but had never been taught to write. It was considered by some to be one of the miracles at Teresa's beatification that Anne learned to write in two days and quickly assumed the role of secretary, taking dictation as Teresa spoke.

So, a loving bond became even stronger. Anne was the faithful companion when Teresa traveled to found new convents and her Holy Mother's support in her final illness. St. Teresa died in Bl. Anne's arms on October 4, 1582.

Sorrow turned to joy when Anne saw Teresa beatified in 1614 and canonized in 1622. But she still had work to do! The little shepherdess, simple lay sister-cum-infirmarian and secretary, left her beloved Spain and helped found houses in France at Tours and Pontoise. When she was elected prioress in Tours she finally had to accept the black veil of choir sister, as Teresa had predicted many years earlier.

Diary of a Country Carmelite

Anne went on to found the Carmel in Antwerp, Belgium and is still venerated there for saving the city from disaster on more than one occasion. She died in 1626 in Antwerp, where she is buried.

In the course of her life she was a prolific writer, composing an autobiography and penning a great body of letters, 665 of which have been preserved for the benefit of those of us who have come after her.

This afternoon, on this beautiful June day, I can see the lilac tree that we planted in Tim's honor after his death. I sit and think, giving thanks for such a day full of memorials. The buds of the lilac have yet to open, they are just tiny ovals of pale green, but they hold the promise of beauty yet to be perceived.

With Blessed Anne at my side and encouraging me, I rest in the certain conviction of the marvel of God's love and in the foretaste of heaven that we are so fortunate to share whenever we receive the Eucharistic Body and Blood of Christ.

This week I had the joy to celebrate Corpus Christi twice, first at a Tridentine Mass on Thursday, where on the old calendar it is observed, and then today at our Novus Ordo Mass. Oh happy coincidence! In Rome, on Thursday Pope Francis celebrated Mass outside in the courtyard of St. John Lateran with thousands in attendance and afterwards led the traditional procession on the Via Merutana, ending at St. Mary Major. He reminded us:

> Today, the feast of Corpus Domini, we have the joy not only of celebrating the mystery, but also of praising Him and singing in the streets of our city. May the procession we will make at the end of Mass, express our gratitude for all the journey that God has allowed us to make through the desert of our poverty, to take us out of slavery, by nourishing us with His love through the Sacrament of his Body and Blood.

My little Ana had this to say some four hundred years earlier:

What infinite love burned in that sacred heart of yours, Lord Jesus! Without uttering a single word you spoke to us; without a word you worked the mysteries you came to accomplish— teaching virtue to the ignorant and blind. What our Lord did was no small thing. Where should we get patience and humility and poverty and the other virtues, and how could we carry each other's burdens and cross, if Christ had not taught us all this first, and given himself as a living model of all perfection?

From poverty to Love!

June 14, 2015

It is a beautiful Sunday afternoon, sunny with a slight breeze. I walk around the garden, admiring the flowers and absorbing the quiet. As I water the plants, I notice that there are some ripe strawberries just asking to be picked. I raise the netting that keeps out the hungry birds and pick just enough berries for dinner. As I bring the brimming bowl to the house, I have a chance to ponder in the silence.

It has been a full week and I am happy to have a day of leisure to remember it all and to properly offer thanks for the gifts it contained.

Monday, Andy and I met at noon with several friends for a Mass being offered for Tim. I must have had the ribbon in my missal in the wrong place for I was surprised by the Reading from the Letter of St. Paul to the Corinthians.

Paul, an Apostle of Christ Jesus by the will of God, and Timothy our brother to the church that is at Corinth.... Blessed be the God and Father of Our Lord Jesus Christ, the Father of compassion and the God of all encouragement, who encourages us in our every affliction with the encouragement with which we ourselves are encouraged by God.

How perfect and uplifting for us, who were there to pray for and remember our Tim. The Gospel continued the personal encouragement for our affliction with a passage from Matthew: Christ teaching on the Mount of the Beatitudes, as it is now called. *"Blessed are the poor in spirit ... Blessed are they who mourn."*

I gave a proper thanksgiving at Communion time, still in the glow of Corpus Christi, for the love of the Heart of Christ and for the Liturgy of the Word which feeds us, too.

After Mass, my friend Dale, another good friend of Tim's, joined me for a picnic lunch in the gazebo at Grandmother's Garden, followed by a stroll among the well-tended flower beds. Taking our cue from St. Paul, we encouraged one another and basked in the joy that true friends share when a day of meeting comes after a long separation.

The week passed with meditations on the Eucharist and the upcoming feast of the Sacred Heart; a week particularly dear to me as Ana Thérèse of the Eucharistic Heart of Jesus. At Mass on Friday, when we celebrated the Solemnity of the Sacred Heart we heard St. Paul again, this time reminding the Ephesians,

> For this reason I kneel before the Father, from whom every family in heaven and on earth is named, that he may grant you in accord with the riches of his glory to be strengthened with power through his Spirit in the inner self, and that Christ may dwell in your hearts through faith; that you, rooted and grounded in love, may have strength to comprehend with all the holy ones what is the breadth and length and height and depth, and to know the love of Christ that surpasses all knowledge, so that you may be filled with all the fullness of God. (Eph. 3:14-19)

Oh, that blessed love that has inspired such a throng of saints—
religious, martyrs and ordinary folk from all walks of life!

On the 12th of June, in years when it doesn't fall on the Solemnity
of the Sacred Heart, we would remember our Carmelite Blessed
Alphonsus Mary of the Holy Spirit Mazurek, who exemplified and
personified that love. Born in Poland in 1891, Alphonsus entered
the Carmelite order in 1905 and eventually was ordained a priest,
fulfilling his role in later years as professor in the Minor Seminary
and prior of his community in Czerna. According to those who
knew him he was not only dedicated to the education of youth, but
had exceptional organizational skills, which he put to good use in
his community.

Living in Poland when it was occupied by the Nazis in the 1940s
was not an easy life. On August 24, 1944, the Nazis invaded the monastery, killing some and forcing others into manual labor. As prior,
Alphonsus was singled out from the rest for particularly gruesome
treatment, and tortured mercilessly. Walking along a dirt road he was
shot, kicked and had dirt forced into his mouth. This was witnessed
by some of his Carmelite friars, who rushed to give him absolution
before he died, rosary in hand. Pope St. John Paul II, who had met
Fr. Alphonsus in Czerna, beatified him in 1999 with a group of other
Polish martyrs, reminding the world that there are those who suffer
persecution for the sake of justice and that *they are often nameless.*

Alphonse relates to us the way to holiness:

All our sanctity and perfection consists in conforming ourselves to the will of God, which is the sole and supreme rule
of perfection and of holiness.

We need not all be preachers, priests, martyrs or do heroic deeds …
only "conform ourselves to the will of God."

How beautiful in its simplicity! His martyrdom was indeed gruesome, but Blessed Alphonsus died as a faithful Catholic priest, doing

God's will, and so we celebrate his life and the place he now occupies with all the holy ones.

To top off the sense of celebration, we had our friend, Maria, as guest on Friday, so my innkeeper's hat and cook's apron were donned to properly offer her our best hospitality. Great feasts are indeed more solemnly and joyfully celebrated with guests around the table.

Maria was with us on Saturday also as we celebrated the feast of the Immaculate Heart of Mary (and St. Anthony!) at Mont Deux Coeurs in Tyringham. It was a perfect day of liturgical celebration as we were present with the Visitation Sisters. It was also the Baptismal anniversary of the celebrant, *and* his ordination anniversary. Double and triple joy! He deftly wove together the threads of the love St. Anthony had for Mary into a homily of whole cloth beauty.

To end this week of feasting, so aptly coming on the heels of Corpus Christi and the Sacred Heart, we have Blessed Maria Candida of the Eucharist, whose feast is June 14th. This little Carmelite was born Maria Barba in Catanzaro, Italy in 1884 and grew up in Palermo, Sicily.

Her life was marked with a love and understanding of the Eucharist that began sweetly at a very young age when she would approach her mother after she came home from daily Mass. Maria would say, "I want God, too!" and prevailed upon her mother to breathe on her, after which she would go away happy, feeling she had accomplished her purpose. Finally, when she was 10, Maria was able to receive her First Communion.

Five years later she developed a deep desire to enter the religious life, but her family objected. For Maria this was a considerable trial but she consoled herself with the Eucharist. When her mother died in 1914, Maria was denied even the consolation of daily Mass and Communion since her brothers would not allow her to go out of the house alone. Finally, when she was 35 she entered Carmel and there continued her "vocation for the Eucharist". She offered herself as a victim: "I ask my Jesus to be a guardian of all the tabernacles of the world until the end of time." Serving as Prioress for almost twenty years, she ruled wisely, left many writings and was responsible for the expansion of the order in Sicily. Sr. Maria Candida of the Eucharist died on June 12, 1949, the Feast of the Holy Trinity. Pope John Paul II beatified her in 2004, calling her an "authentic mystic" and "tireless apostle of the Eucharist". How fitting that one of the miracles put forth for her beatification would be a multiplication of hosts during Holy Mass!

May Blessed Maria Candida inspire a great number of souls to truly appreciate and value the immense gift of Christ among us.

> I do not know how to separate the ciborium in the sacred Tabernacle from the ciborium in our hearts!
> What mystery of love is this intimacy with our Beloved! I reflect on this sometimes with emotion, and give praise to Him Who is love! (Blessed Maria Candida of the Eucharist)

June 29, 2015

From inside on the screen porch I have a panoramic view on three sides. The maple trees flutter their leaves as the breeze picks up and then dies down; the birds cycle their own individual songs over and over as the sun lets in a little light when it can find an opening in the clouds.

We have had a bit of rain lately and this morning I "squish, squashed" my way back to the vegetable and fruit gardens. I thinned some apples on our trees, checked for ripe raspberries … not quite … and found a place for some astilbe plants that were a gift from my neighbor, Linda. Another quiet day at home.

I am without my car again today; this time it is the rear brakes that need replacing. So instead of going to Mass I pause in the afternoon to read the Epistles and Gospel of the day and quietly make a Spiritual Communion. It is the Solemnity of Saints Peter and Paul and I would have loved to go to Mass today, but "no wheels" and no one else in Blandford heading there. So, I rest in God's will and make the best of it. There is beauty here, and a stillness comparable to a quiet church and I can find God in any place ... in my work and in my resting. *"The praise of God shall be ever upon my lips."* (Psalm 34).

It is traditionally a day set aside to pray for the Church, so I add my prayers, but also my digging and trimming, my sewing and washing of dishes, the act of putting clean sheets upon the bed, the chopping of vegetables and coring of strawberries to the lifting up of hearts in all corners of the world that we might all be humble and tireless apostles, produce holy priests and bishops and offer a great hymn of thanksgiving for the gift of the Catholic Church.

O God, who on the Solemnity of the Apostles Peter and Paul give us the noble and holy joy of this day, grant, we pray, that your Church may in all things follow the teaching of those through whom she received the beginnings of right religion. Through our Lord Jesus Christ, your Son, who lives and reigns with you in the unity of the Holy Spirit, one God forever and ever. Amen.

July

July 7, 2015

The big push to plant and nurture along the vegetable garden has eased up a bit by now. We are enjoying lettuce, green beans and fresh herbs and it won't be long before we will have several varieties of tomatoes ripe enough to pick.

The small fruits—strawberries and raspberries—are another matter. Both beds are more productive than I have ever seen them and the challenge is to pick often enough and to have a plan for using the berries soon or preserving them. Yesterday I picked about three pints of raspberries in the early evening that will be baked into a pie. Andy's favorite!

The great abundance in this growing season mirrors the abundance of Carmelite feasts in July. We have seven holy ones to commemorate, but also on the calendar is the feast of Our Lady of Mount Carmel. Today we begin our novena to better prepare for the celebration of this great feast of Mary.

"*O, Beautiful Flower of Carmel, most fruitful vine*", the novena starts out. What perfect images for this season of bounty when each plant has its own budding forth and then, fruiting. As we apply the images and titles to Mary we see the exquisite beauty of her being … body and soul … but also her spiritual gifts and the "fruit of her womb, Jesus."

Beauty, while holding perfection in and of itself, is fulfilling its purpose in fruitfulness. We must not be content to remain only an image or portrait of the Divine Essence. We must, as Mary did, come to perfection in the natural progression of bearing fruit … our faith and good works … the only fruit that will last.

July 8, 2015

I went to noon Mass in Westfield today, arriving early for my half hour of mental prayer and then praying the Office of Readings afterward. It is good to have at least one day a week when there are no commitments or appointments on the calendar and I can draw out my visits to Church.

Later, back on the hill at home, I feel the pull of an old familiar yearning. Checking the clock, I realize that I have about forty minutes that could be spent outside. The morning's humidity has moderated somewhat and the intermittent breeze and cloud cover have made it a most pleasant afternoon.

I grab my trowel and little kneeling mat and head for the circular flower bed near the raspberries. The dwarf Japanese maple in the center of the bed provides extra shade as I inspect the little zinnia seedlings. Using the point of the trowel, I dig out some weeds that are starting to choke the small flower plants. This type of weeding, unhurried and concentrated on one small area, is so contemplative! I am already in the posture of prayer and it is so natural to praise God when His lavish beauty is all about me. The birds are providing the background music and the chickens the moments of drama. One hen has just laid an egg judging from her loud and prolonged cackling.

Out come the wild violets and three or four other types of weeds that I can't name. The ground cover astilbe now has room to spread its roots without the obstructions the weeds presented. It's a small plant and will bloom at the end of summer sending up short pink feather-like spikes.

The comparisons to the spiritual life come unbidden. Like most gardens, the beauty within comes about through the dint of hard work and constant weeding. Persistently working on those habitual, ingrained, deeply-rooted, weedy faults and sins ... pulling them out by the roots and not growing weary of the effort; letting the master Gardener prune us through trials, cutting away the dead wood of all attachments and fertilizing and watering with His grace and sweet Presence.

And, in the Garden is Mary, "Queen, Beauty of Carmel". We place ourselves in her hands as the protector and mother of our interior life. Today, on the second day of the novena, I ask her to help me dig deep to find the roots of those weeds which are preventing my growth in the spiritual life and, with her strength and gentle persistence, to dig them out once and for all, so that I, too, may bloom in the garden.

July 13, 2015

After a string of busy days, it is so good to have some time to slow down. I begin the day with the best remedy, morning Mass, then straighten up the house, all the while de-cluttering the mind and opening up more space for recollection.

In the creative realm, I help my neighbor Linda design a label for the quilt we've been working on for her daughter. I show her an applique technique for the vintage umbrella square that will document the history of the quilt, then send her off to work on it.

Finally, I manage to make my way outside. I dead-head some flowers, water and fertilize the transplants and vegetables and, while pulling up some weeds in a bed behind the barn, I marvel all over again at the beauty and variety just in this small space. Daylilies and lupine, bright yellow calendula and small English daisies are all blooming today. Some annuals I started from seed—marigold and venidium—are filling out and will flower soon. A group of new lilies are gifts from Linda's garden. They are tall, but as yet an unknown beauty, as are the gladioli and begonias that will burst forth once their bulbs and tubers come to maturity. There is a bright pink mandevilla, a vacationing southerner, that is quite exquisite right now.

All the myriad varieties, colors, textures and forms speak to me of the infinite creativity of the designer. How can one doubt the existence and goodness of God in a garden? St. Teresa Benedicta of the Cross expresses my sentiments in several lines from a poem:

> *How wonderful are your gracious wonders!*
> *All we can do is be amazed and stammer and fall silent,*
> *Because intellect and words fail.*
> (St. Teresa Benedicta of the Cross, *I Will*
> *Remain with You*)

Today we celebrate the first of July's bouquet of Carmelite saints, Teresa of the Andes, a young Carmelite from Chile who was canonized by Pope St. John Paul II in 1993.

Juanita Fernandez Solar was born on this day in Santiago in the year 1900, the fifth child of a wealthy, Catholic family. She was particularly close to her brothers and sisters but had some serious faults to overcome in the arms of that family. By her own admission, she had to conquer her pride, control her anger, learn obedience and calm an overly-sensitive nature.

Her parents and grandparents helped, as did the Sacred Heart sisters at the convent school she attended. Like a number of other saints, she was devout from an early age and greatly desired to receive Jesus in Holy Communion. Juanita prepared for a year in advance with the aid of Mary. "During that time the Virgin helped to purify my heart from all imperfections," she recounts. What maturity for a ten-year-old!

Juanita was not a brilliant student, but progressed with hard work as the years went on. She read *The Story of a Soul* when she was fourteen and felt drawn to Thérèse of Lisieux, who was yet to be beatified. She also suffered greatly during surgery for appendicitis in the same year and afterward underwent a period of deep sorrow at having to leave her family to board at school. Through a diary she kept, we have the blessing to follow along as she progresses in the spiritual life. Juanita heard the call of Christ to her Carmelite vocation, made a private vow of chastity and showed a preferential charity in her love for struggling classmates, her neighbors on the family estate and in the care she lavished on one particular poor little boy, whom she helped to feed and clothe.

When her father's financial problems resulted in the loss of the estate, Juanita saw a call to detachment and readily gave up the life she had been accustomed to living. The writings of another young Carmelite, Elizabeth of the Trinity, influenced her at this time and she advanced further in the life of grace, striving to live always in the awareness of the presence of God. Her brother Lucho called her "the jewel of the house"!

Juanita finally left school to help in the family home, but amid this ordinary life with its periods of swimming, tennis and marveling at nature, she took the next step in pursuing her vocation with a visit to the Carmel of Los Andes.

Recognizing in this spot her true home, she penned a letter to her father in March of 1919, asking permission to enter the convent. Permission was granted and in May she began her postulancy as Sister Teresa of Jesus.

For one so close to her family, the separation was painful but she embraced the Carmelite life with great joy, seeing as her goals:

1. To Love
2. To Suffer
3. To Pray, especially for the conversion of sinners, the sanctification of priests and the Church.

Diary of a Country Carmelite

What is the life of a Carmelite if not one of contemplating, adoring and loving God incessantly? And she, by being desirous for that heaven, distances herself as much as possible from everything earthly.

The house of Bethany was the delight of Jesus when He was on earth; it was His favorite dwelling. There He was intimately known by Lazarus, served by Martha and madly loved by Mary. The Carmelite being close to Jesus reproduces that intimate life now. She learns to love Him and serve Him according to His will. She is His refuge in the midst of the world, she with His chosen ones is His favorite dwelling place. (St. Teresa of the Andes, *Diary*)

She donned the Carmelite habit in October, but the following spring she became very ill and had a premonition of her own death. Seeing her so sick, the Superior allowed Sr. Teresa of Jesus to profess her vows on April 7th. Just five days later, she died of advanced typhus. Her community was stunned and in mourning but began to see the breadth of her influence when the funeral was held and the crowds of mourners came from near and far and graces were bestowed. Later that year her sister Rebecca entered Los Andes to follow in Teresa's footsteps.

A million make their way to her shrine in Rinconada, Chile each year, coming to know her through her diary and the letters she left behind. Her mission is to get *them* to know God, to love Him and to make their lives a continual silent prayer.

As Pope St. John XXIII reminds us:

God desires us to follow the examples of the saints by absorbing the vital sap of their virtues and turning it into our own life-blood, adapting it to our own individual capacities and particular circumstances.

May our little Teresita of the Andes help us to follow her example in all things and reap the rich reward of union with God here and hereafter.

Today on the 7th day of our novena to Our Lady of Mt. Carmel, we pray to Mary, Help of Christians and ask her to protect and aid us. *"May all that we do be pleasing to your Son and to you."*

In seeing you, Virgin Mary so pure, so tender, and so compassionate, who would not be encouraged to unburden his intimate sufferings to you? Who would not ask you to be his star on this stormy sea? (St. Teresa of the Andes, *Diary*)

July 15, 2015

Our granddaughter, Kateri, had dinner with us last night to celebrate the feast of her patron, St. Kateri Tekakwitha, and then spent the night so she and I could go shopping and out to lunch today to redeem her birthday "Groupon". (In our family that means "Granny Coupon"!)

But, of course, first was a drive into town this morning to start the day off right with Holy Mass. I had some lovely conversations in the car with Kateri, who just turned seven, that gave me a little glimpse into her beautiful, simple faith.

As if on cue, the Gospel this morning reminded us again of the words of Jesus:

I give praise to you, Father, Lord of heaven and earth. For although you have hidden these things from the wise and learned you have revealed them to the childlike (Mt 11:25).

On this last day of our novena to Our Lady, we beg Mary's intercession as her children and ask her to "Look down mercifully ... on all those who do not know that they are numbered among your children". They are many and scattered far and wide. We have that serious responsibility to pray for them. And today we add a day of fast to our prayers.

Diary of a Country Carmelite

This evening I make my way outside to the garden, fresh and full of beauty after a summer rain. I pray Evening Prayer I for the Solemnity in front of the Mary Garden with the hymn, psalms, antiphons and reading particular to the vigil. In the Intercessions we pray:

You have made Mary the Mother of our race, and urge us with her help
to dedicate our lives to you and the service of our brothers and sisters
    —may we be worthy to be called her children, always seek your face,
and be untiring in our work for the salvation of all.

Amen!

July 16, 2015

O Mary, Queen, Beauty of Carmel! The day of fasting having prepared us in body and spirit, we celebrate, the world over, our Lady and Queen.

I make the rounds of the flower beds in the early morning, cutting some hosta leaves, cosmos, veronica, feverfew and calendula. After arranging my armful of stems into a simple bouquet, I drive in the silence to morning Mass at the Visitation Monastery in Tyringham. Lee and I share the beauty of the same liturgy with the sisters and hear a homily that would put a smile on any Carmelite face. Oh, how blessed we are to have this sacred liturgy so accessible in our part of the world!

After Mass we give each other the greetings of the day and I present the bouquet to her before we go our separate ways.

When my day at the library is over I treat myself to an afternoon in the garden, having a gem of a perfect day and the silence … finally … that I have been craving. I ponder and pray, the words of Fr. Gabriel from this morning's meditation presenting themselves again, in the shade of the afternoon garden:

> Those who wish to live truly devoted to Our Lady of Mount Carmel, must follow Mary into the depths of the interior life. Carmel is the symbol of the contemplative life, of life wholly consecrated to seeking God and tending wholly toward divine intimacy; and she who best realizes this ideal is Mary, Queen, Beauty of Carmel. (Fr. Gabriel of St. Mary Magdalen, OCD, *Divine Intimacy*, 378)

Alone in my garden I "see" the photo Fr. Tom sent from Rome today, when he happened upon a procession of Carmelite friars bearing a regal statue of Our Lady of Mount Carmel through the streets. All of us, priests and nuns in their monasteries and we seculars scattered in our homes throughout the world, follow along bearing her train and feeling the benediction of her motherly graces upon our bowed heads.

> May the most holy Virgin Mary confirm you in your Carmelite vocation. May she safeguard your love for the things of the spirit. May she obtain for you the graces you need in your holy, laborious ascent toward the knowledge of the divine realm and the ineffable experiences of its dark nights and light filled days. May she give you the desire for sanctity, the desire to bear eschatological witness to the kingdom of heaven. May she make you models for the members of God's Church, united closely to them. And may she one day lead you into that possession of Christ and his glory which, even now, is the goal toward which your whole life is directed. (Second Reading, Office of Readings, July 16, from Addresses by Pope Paul VI, June 22, 1967)

Deo Gratias!

Diary of a Country Carmelite

July 17, 2015

I tidied up the house this morning and started some bread dough, putting it in the warm oven to rise. Our grandson, Nicholas, is coming to stay with us for four days so I am making sure the house is in readiness and that there is a plan for meals that include some of his favorites. Hospitality demands this of me and I am happy to provide it.

I managed to squeeze in a little time in the garden, using the quiet and solitude to calm myself and rest in the presence of God.

At the back of my mind, though, are a group of Carmelites from Compiegne who are to be the subjects of my writing today. I have admired them for years but am wondering how in my busy day I will find the time to research the details of their story and get it all down on paper. As most worries usually are, this one is groundless and the solution comes from an unexpected quarter.

Sitting down at the computer for a moment's pause after my work in the garden, I find an email from my friend, Suzie, a fellow Carmelite who lives in California. She suddenly felt moved to send two of us a message highlighting the very story I was to recount, complete with a link to an excellent article about the French martyrs. With a sudden and profound gratitude, I smile and thank God for this gift, presented in my need.

The Carmelites from Compiegne have been memorialized in literature and opera, with not a few historic accounts of their story written as well. They have inspired so many by their heroic deaths, offered, like St. Teresa Benedicta's, who was herself inspired by them, as holocaust to end the horrors of the French Revolution.

In November, 1789, religious orders in France were outlawed, monasteries closed, church property confiscated and religious dispersed among the laity. It was a crime against the revolutionary government to dress as a nun or priest and to live in community. You cannot take the faith away from those dedicated to God, however, and though they dressed in common clothing, the Carmelite sisters of Compiegne attracted the attention of the thugs in power. They were arrested in June of 1794 along with other religious, but remained calm and prayerful, praying daily that they could give their lives for an end to the Terror. Sr. Teresa of St. Augustine, the prioress, and her fellow choir sisters, lay sisters and externs had their deepest wishes confirmed when they were condemned to death without the benefit of a proper trial. Mother Henriette of Jesus, a former prioress, spoke up and demanded that in addition to the trumped-up charges for which they had been arrested, should be added "attachment to your Religion and the King". When her request was granted, she beamed and spoke to her sisters in the community, "We must rejoice and give thanks to God for we die for our religion, our faith, and for being members of the Holy Roman Catholic Church." She wanted everyone to be clear about the real reason for their condemnation.

After several days of uncertainty in prison, the prioress, Mother Teresa of St. Augustine, knowing the stress her daughters would be under on the day of execution, arranged to trade a fur collar for 17 cups of chocolate. What a tender and thoughtful mother, seeing to the needs of her children!

On July 17, they made their way by cart to the guillotine in Paris. The usually unruly mob on hand to gape at the atrocities were soon silenced by the quiet and peaceful sisters, who each kissed a tiny statue of the Madonna in the hands of their prioress, asked for her blessing and her permission to die and then mounted the steps to a death offered to God in expiation for the sins of the government. Together they sang, giving praise to God; their voices getting quieter as they decreased in number, but giving no less an example to the watching crowds.

Remarkably, in human terms, the Reign of Terror ended ten short days later. Their offering was accepted and bore fruit abundantly.

These "enemies of the people", along with all the other martyrs of the French Revolution, became the sacred army which obtained the real freedom of France from tyranny.

> Amid the stench of that festering site in the City of Lights, humanity was that evening reduced to an inexplicable silence, respectfully maintained till the end of the immolation, while those being immolated praised God for confirming his mercy upon them through this action. Could there be a better witness that the banished Christian God had not been banished at all, but was even then stooping to touch, not only the sixteen victims, but also all present at that place of sacrifice with something of his glory, that "glory of the only-begotten of the Father, full of grace and truth."(Jn 1:14)?
>
> The world can never contain the glory of Jesus Christ, for it is not of this world. Yet, even so, in the Father's great mercy to our fallen race through the Holy Spirit, the glory of the only-begotten Son can be seen and experienced by those who, in self-imposed silence, participated in the theophany which constituted the martyrdom of the sixteen Carmelites of Compiegne. (William Bush, *To Quell the Terror*)

Mother Teresa of St. Augustine and her fifteen companions were beatified in 1906, the first group of martyrs from the period, and their story continues to be told and to inspire others to great generosity.

Mother Teresa of St. Augustine, *ora pro nobis.*
Mother Teresa of Jesus, *ora pro nobis.*
Mother St. Louis, *ora pro nobis.*
Sister Mary of Jesus Crucified, *ora pro nobis.*
Sister Charlotte of the Resurrection, *ora pro nobis.*
Sister Teresa of the Holy Heart of Mary, *ora pro nobis.*
Mother Henriette of Jesus, *ora pro nobis.*

Sister Teresa of St. Ignatius, *ora pro nobis.*
Sister Julia Louis of Jesus, *ora pro nobis.*
Sister Mary Henrietta of Providence, *ora pro nobis.*
Sister Euphrasia of the Immaculate Conception, *ora pro nobis.*
Sister Constance, *ora pro nobis.*
Sister Mary of the Holy Ghost, *ora pro nobis.*
Sister St. Martha, *ora pro nobis.*
Sister St. Francis Xavier, *ora pro nobis.*
Catherine Soiren, *ora pro nobis.*
Teresa Soiren, *ora pro nobis.*

What a story I have to tell Nicholas this evening!

July 20, 2015

I love waking early on a summer morning! Even when the alarm rings at five a.m. it is already light and I move about in the coolness of the new day, settling in on the breezy porch for meditation and Morning Prayer.

Today, another feast! We have the beauty of our Carmelite Propers to pray; the hymns, readings and even the intercessions on this day commemorating St. Elijah, are ripe with meaning:

> *Lord, you revealed yourself to the prophet Elijah in silence and solitude,*
> —*help us to put aside all that can prevent us from hearing your voice,*
> *so that we may seek you unceasingly until we find you.*

And

> *Lord, you revealed yourself to Elijah in the murmuring of a gentle breeze,*
> —*may we learn silence and docility to perceive the slightest breathing*
> *of the Holy Spirit.*

Diary of a Country Carmelite

We pray to Elijah, father and spiritual model of the original brothers upon Mount Carmel, now the model for us as Carmelites in all the ways of prayer.

Almighty, ever-living God, your prophet Elijah, our Father, lived always in your presence and was zealous for the honor due to your name. May we, your servants, always seek your face and bear witness to your love. We ask this through Our Lord Jesus Christ, your Son, who lives and reigns with you and the Holy Spirit, one God, for ever and ever. Amen.

With Elijah's zeal, I go about my day, cultivating silence as well as my vegetables and making that strong effort to hear in the breeze of the Holy Spirit the plan for this new day as I bear witness to that love.

July 23, 2015

After my day at the library, I head to a little Mennonite bakery and deli to pick up some sandwiches and cookies, then meet Andy in Westfield where we travel together for a rare night out. It is a lovely drive along the Connecticut River past farmland and vegetable stands, then a switch-back, up and up to the top of Mount Holyoke, finding at the end of the road "Summit House", ready and waiting for tonight's concert.

We park ourselves on an empty bench on the porch and there, enjoying our picnic, marvel at the spectacular view before us of cultivated land, river and hills that we had just driven through. It is another perfect summer day, complete with gentle breeze, and we feel so blessed to be able to take some time apart from our busy days to stop and savor it.

It also sets the stage to contemplate the spiritual realities of this day. With this beauty spread at our feet we thank God for Mary, Mother of Divine Grace, our Mother, too, in the order of grace and as the

Mother of Christ, the fount from which that grace springs. What a gift and beauty, what a Mother to be honored and appreciated under so many titles.

We file into the old building at concert time and sit back to listen to "Zoe Darrow and the Fiddleheads"; the fiddle, guitar and keyboard filling us with another particular sort of beauty. This hilltop venue provides the perfect tradition at just the right moment for intermission. Several minutes before sunset we all leave our chairs and head outside to the porch railing to glimpse the beauty of the sunset. How radiantly stunning! As I look over to my left I see a grassy knoll and outcropping of rock and a memory comes flooding back from our homeschooling days.

We had hiked up the mountain with a group of friends and then at the top, transformed from hikers into congregation, we witnessed the greatest act of grace—the Holy Mass celebrated by a young priest holding up the Host—Jesus Christ—Creator and Redeemer of this world of beauty, for us to adore and receive.

Praying Evening Prayer now in honor of the Mother of this Lord, I sing with a lilt of Scottish fiddle playing in the background,

God of eternal wisdom, in your providence
you willed that the Blessed Virgin Mary
should bring forth the Author of Grace,
and take part with him in the mystery of our redemption.
May she obtain for us grace in abundance
and bring us to the haven of everlasting salvation.

July 24, 2015

The yellow and green summer squash have begun to appear and the flower beds are lush, too. Sadly, so are the weeds. The abundance of summer, of harvest and of beauty keeps me busy again today, as I work to maintain it all.

Once again, too, I take another nosegay from July's bouquet of feasts and saints. Today we Carmelites celebrate two groups of Spanish martyrs from that ugly period of Spain's civil war. One group of three comes from Guadalajara during the time when, as in France in the late 1700s with the martyrs of Compiegne, the religious orders were commanded to disperse and to dress in secular clothes. The sisters obeyed, kept a low profile and often moved to safer quarters when they felt threatened.

Blesseds Maria Pilar of St. Francis Borgia, Teresa of the Child Jesus and St. John of the Cross, and Maria Angeles of St. Joseph all found themselves in such a situation in the summer of 1936. They were not strangers to holiness or to valor, though.

Maria Pilar was 58, but like her fellow Carmelites had been called to Carmel at a young age. She loved the silence of the convent and spending time in adoration with "The Living One", as she called Jesus, reposed in the monstrance.

Teresa, 27, felt the pull of Carmel as young as thirteen and was given permission to enter at sixteen. She, too, loved her time before the Blessed Sacrament, calling it "sunbathing". She was happy to be tired after a long day's work, treating her fellow Carmelites with "charity above all", as she expressed in her motto.

Maria Angeles, 31, was 24 when she entered Carmel and was admired for her fervent missionary spirit and remembered for her holiness by the prioress who called her a "little angel".

These three knew the perilous times in which they lived and had promised to offer themselves as victims for an end to the persecution. On this day in 1936, while moving to a safer place to live, they were apprehended and shot, giving a bold witness to their faith. They were beatified by Pope John Paul II in 1987.

Meanwhile, in Barcelona a similar situation was playing out. Maria Mercedes Prat, 56, was recognized as a religious while on an errand with another sister from her community. After being interrogated and tortured, she was finally shot along with her companion, who lived to be a witness to Maria Mercedes' beatification.

Growing up as a child who loved God particularly, even at a young age, she saw her own faith tested with the death of her father when she was fifteen and her mother a year later. As the eldest of four children, it was her responsibility to keep the family intact. After fulfilling this obligation, she entered the convent and became Maria Mercedes of the Sacred Heart, teaching painting and needlework among other things, until that fateful day in 1936 when she was forced to pronounce her final lesson in love. Her companion, Sr. Giocchina Miguel, heard her last testimony to her faith, the praying of the Apostles Creed and then the Our Father. She died after uttering the words, *as we forgive those who trespass against us.* Maria Mercedes was beatified by Pope John Paul II in 1990.

Continuing on with the image of a bouquet or garland of flowers, we hear St. John of the Cross in the Office of Readings from the martyrs of Guadalajara:

> Each holy soul is like a garland adorned with the flowers of virtues and gifts, and all of them together form a garland for the head of Christ, the Bridegroom.
>
> The loving garlands can refer to what we call aureoles; these are also woven by Christ, the Bridegroom.

He mentions that of virgins, then holy doctors and ...

> the third is fashioned from the crimson carnations of the martyrs....
>
> The flower of these works and virtues is the grace and power they possess from the love of God. Without love their works will not only fail to flower, but they will all wither and become valueless in God's sight, even though they may be

perfect from a human standpoint. Yet because God bestows his grace and love, they are works that have blossomed in his love. (St. John of the Cross, *Spiritual Canticle*, Strophe 30, 7-8)

Making the rounds of the flower beds before dinner, I cut some of the prettiest blooms and arrange them in a vase for the dinner table, a simple reminder of the virtue and sacrifice of these holy women. May they inspire us all to live faithfully in whatever witness we are called upon to make.

July 26, 2015

We have the great pleasure to sit with our son Paul and our two granddaughters at Mass this Sunday, while Nicholas serves at the altar. A little hand makes its way into mine as we pray and wait quietly for the music to begin.

Many honor this day as Catholic Grandparents' Day, which is most fitting as it is the feast of Saints Joachim and Anne, the parents of Mary. As Carmelites we also honor these grandparents of Jesus as Protectors of Carmel, second only to St. Joseph in this role. For those of us who have been grandparents for some time, the idea of protection is a familiar one.

As Joachim and Anne fulfilled this role with valor while tending their holy daughter, Mary, so now we pray to them for protection for all Carmelites. May they keep us holy and faithful to our vocations, always striving to be good sons and daughters of Mary, Queen and Beauty of Carmel.

> *Lord, God of our fathers and mothers,*
> *you bestowed on Saint Joachim and Saint Anne*
> *the singular grace that their daughter, Mary,*

should become the Mother of your Son, Jesus Christ.
Grant, at their intercession,
the salvation you promised to your people.
We make our prayer through Christ our Lord.
Amen.

How blessed are the parents of the Mother of God. The whole world is indebted to them: the prophets, because their prophecies concerning the Incarnation of Christ are fulfilled; the Apostles, because thanks to the daughter of these two saints they have become children of the light; the holy martyrs, because they owe their crown to them; the saints and holy ones, because they will be able to inherit future good things; sinners because the prayers of the Mother of God will obtain mercy for them. (St. Cosmas of Maiuma)

July 27, 2015

It has been one of those volatile summer days with periods of sun but also a heavy humidity that is markedly uneasy. Though we haven't had rain yet, there has been rolling thunder in the distance and dark clouds on the horizon that portend a heavy storm.

The gathering clouds make me think of Blessed Titus Brandsma, today's Carmelite, and the most volatile years in which he lived.

Born in 1881 in the Netherlands and ordained a Carmelite priest in 1905, Titus most likely had a number of peaceful years, earning his doctorate in philosophy, teaching and serving in various capacities in the Carmelite Order. He was also a perceptive man and, undoubtedly, saw the storm clouds gathering in Germany with the rise of the Nazi Party and its ideology that was so contrary to the Gospel. The Nazis occupied the Netherlands in 1940 and to mitigate their influence, the bishops of Holland appointed Fr. Titus to be a spiritual advisor to the country's Catholic newspaper editors. He voiced his opposition to any collusion with the Nazis in the Catholic press and in 1941 met with each editor to explain why it was impossible for them to comply with the edict to print Nazi propaganda and advertisements. For this he was eventually arrested and traded his monastery cell for a bunk in a concentration camp.

He was a faithful friar to the end, serving his congregation of fellow prisoners and even his captors. Death came in Dachau in 1942, but it was no defeat for our stalwart priest, only the opening of a door into eternal happiness with the Lord whom he loved and served.

His story and the era in which he lived have so many comparisons to our own time.

Christians still suffer persecution and martyrdom in countries all over the globe. And closer to home, we see the religious freedom that Blessed Titus Brandsma championed being eroded through laws and legal decisions. It is time for another group of brave "Christian soldiers" to hold fast with prayer, reason and argument to fight the decline of our culture and the loss of morality.

You hear it said that we live in a wonderful time, a time of great men and women. It would probably be better to say that we live in an era of decadence in which many, however, feel the need to react and defend that which is most precious and sacred....

In our better moments, however, we do recognize our imperfections and then we understand that there is room for improvement. We are honestly convinced that we could improve if we had more courage. Nothing is accomplished without effort, without struggle. In our better moments we no longer shed tears over our own weaknesses or over those of others, but we recall what was interiorly said to St. Paul: My grace is sufficient for you: in union with me you can do all things.

... We shall not give up on love. Love will gain back for us the hearts of these pagans. Nature is stronger than theory; let theory condemn and reject love and call it weakness; the living witness of love will always renew the power which will capture the hearts of men. (Blessed Titus Brandsma, *Sermons*, Alternative Second Reading, Office of Readings)

May we all beg the help of Blessed Titus to continue our struggle to live and give testimony, with heroic courage, to the charity and the faith for which he gave his life.

July 28, 2015

This was *supposed* to be a red-letter day! Andy and I both had the day off of work, our plans were made ... and then ... somewhere on the other side of the world, Amsterdam to be precise (I'm sure Blessed Titus Brandsma has been there!), an airplane has a radio malfunction. So, instead of driving to Boston to pick up our son, Fr. Thomas, from the airport, we are at home.

Fr. Tom walks the streets of Amsterdam, sightseeing and having conversations with people he would otherwise never have met, and we finally take advantage of an unscheduled day to borrow a movie from the library and bring home a pizza from the little country store across the street. With good grace we accept the change in plans and pray that tomorrow he will find a flight home.

The Carmelite whose memorial we celebrate today, Blessed John Soreth, must have had his share of travel problems, I'd wager. Being born in the middle of the 15th century, though, they probably had more to do with blisters, highwaymen, horses gone lame or broken cart wheels.

John was a native of Normandy and studied at the University of Paris. As a Carmelite he was quite concerned about the abuses that had crept into the Order. He was elected Prior General of the Carmelites in 1451 and set about to put things right. He wrote new constitutions and traveled far and wide visiting monasteries to preach to the friars in his urgent but gentle way. He encouraged them to remain faithful to prayer and to follow through with their vows of poverty. As is often the case with a prophet or reformer, his admonitions were mostly ignored.

Some things haven't changed over the centuries! Sin and obstinance are always with us.

John kept on, however, along the path that God had set him on. He also began the foundation for the Second Order, Carmelite nuns, establishing houses in half a dozen cities in the Netherlands (there's that connection again), France, and Italy. Happily, for all of us seculars, he had the vision to see that lay men and women could also benefit from a life of Carmelite spirituality.

John continued the reform for twenty years until his death in 1471. Teresa of Avila, born in 1515, cited John Soreth as a particular protector of the Order, especially during the turmoil of the Protestant Reformation, which arose in 1517 with the posting of Martin Luther's list.

Blessed John is often pictured holding a ciborium, which represents a particular incident of faith and bravery in his life. In the city of Liege, a violent mob stormed a church and desecrated the Blessed Sacrament, strewing hosts all over the floor. Undaunted, John picked them all up and carried them safely to a Carmelite church.

With the prayers and example of Blessed John Soreth before us and all around us, let us listen to his words and follow in his footsteps.

So let the love of Christ inflame your zeal, pervade your knowledge, and confirm your steadfastness. Let it be fervent, circumspect and unbowed, not lukewarm or undiscerning. Love the Lord your God with all the affection of which your heart is capable; love him with all the watchfulness, all the circumspection of your soul, or rather your reason; love him with all your strength so that you may not fear even death for the sake of his love. Let our Lord Jesus Christ be so sweet to your affections that he will repel the sweet allurements of the flesh: let sweetness himself conquer sweetness. But let him also be the guiding light of your intellect, the ruler of your reason, so that you may not only escape the snares of heresy's deceptions and protect your faith from their subtleties, but also carefully avoid undue or indiscreet vehemence in your behavior. (Blessed John Soreth, *Exhortation on the Carmelite Rule*)

July 29, 2015

Fr. Tom has a flight to Boston today, though I have a momentary panic when it is also delayed by several hours. I use the extra time to bake some cookies and mix up some more dough to have on hand for later. We pick up our granddaughter, Bella, for the 2-hour trip to the airport. I, for one, am happy to have her sweet nine-year old, optimistic presence with us as we arrive at Logan and try to translate the airport direction signs. On our second loop around we finally find the right parking area for our terminal and make our way to the international arrival gate.

We don't have long to wait before we catch a glimpse of a tall blonde with glasses in clerical garb. Joy! Oh, sweet and happy reunion! It has been a year since we have seen our son and three years since he has been home. He truly is a sight for sore eyes.

We hear all about Amsterdam on the ride home—the parts of the city Fr. Tom had time to walk through, the canals, the cold drizzle and the conversations and interactions he would otherwise have missed if his plane had left yesterday. More instances of the eternal goodness of God and His work in the circumstances of our lives. *Omnia in Bonum!*

When we get home, we ready ourselves and the living room for the celebration of Mass. Out comes a small table, a white altar cloth, candles, flowers, crucifix and all that is necessary. Paul arrives with the rest of the children and we compose ourselves to participate in the most solemn celebration of Holy Mass.

Today is the Memorial of St. Martha, and Andy reads for us from the letter of St. John, the eloquent "marching orders" (1 John 4:7) that every family, every individual is called to obey:

> Beloved, let us love one another, because love is of God: every-one who loves is begotten by God and knows God. Whoever is without love does not know God, for God is love.

The father of our family lays it out for us in simplicity and urgency.

> Whoever acknowledges that Jesus is the Son of God, God remains in Him and he in God.

Psalm 34 tells us what is in store for those who so remain: we will be delivered from our fears, radiant with joy, saved from all distress and lacking nothing!

We rise when Fr. Tom does and hear about Martha and Mary, one anxious and harried, one at peace and receptive. Then we sit and do our best to follow Mary's example while with perfect simplicity and in words accessible to the little ones and their elders we hear our son, brother and uncle, but our Father, too, open up the words of the Gospel for us. Like this Biblical family, "Christ has come into our house today!" We must listen and then ask Him, "What do you want me to do?"

Then Christ is *really* come! We gaze upon Him with the eyes of faith and become one with Him as we kneel and receive His sacred humanity and divinity. One with Christ, one with each other, one with all those who have gone before us, played and prayed in this room. Too soon the moment ends, the candles are extinguished and we work on preparing another sort of meal.

We are changed forever and strengthened with this eternal food, this daily bread, for the next day, the next crisis, the next temptation.

We give Thee thanks, Almighty God, for all thy graces and blessings, who livest and reignest forever and ever, world without end. Amen.

July 31, 2015

Today, Fr. Tom and I pray Lauds and the Office of Readings in the car on the way to Mass. This morning is a concelebrated Mass with Fr. Chris at St. Mary's. The two young priests had a chance to meet over dinner last night and it was evident that they share the same love of God and zeal for souls.

In the sanctuary of the basement chapel we see them interact in a different way: joined together in offering to the Father the death and resurrection of the Son. Fr. Tom preaches about St. Ignatius of Loyola, the saint whose feast is on the calendar today, and encourages us to follow his example and devote sufficient time and energy to all our "spiritual exercises" and not to relegate them to second place after our exertions in the other areas of our lives.

Back at the ranch, Andy, Fr. Tom and I work together on our entry in the "Great Pie Contest": a raspberry apple pie with a cream cheese layer, our contribution to the celebration for Paul's birthday. It is like old times to have the kitchen busy with peeling, cutting and slicing.

Diary of a Country Carmelite

Once again, in the evening I have company for the praying of Vespers ... what a joy! As we sit on the porch with an evening breeze stirring the air gently, the two of us pray together and also with a host of others around the globe. We praise God and beg Him to stir our hearts into action for His glory and for the needs of all our brothers and sisters. Our family has been enriched with two more today as our grandnephew and grandniece, tiny twins, Bryce Gregory and Alexa Grace, have been born.

> *Mighty and wonderful are your works, Lord God Almighty!*
> *Righteous and true are your ways, O King of the nations!*
> (Canticle, Evening Prayer, Friday, Week 1)

August

August 1, 2015

This morning I wake early to bake bread and put all in readiness for our drive north to Hampton, New York, where my mother and father live. As I head outside to let the chickens out of the barn, I see the full moon setting in the mists of morning. What a glorious day!

We find room in the car to pack all our suitcases and supplies and head out for the three-hour trip, so reminiscent of countless other family outings. Mom and Dad welcome us at the door of their log cabin and before anything else we prepare the "great room" for its highest function. Table becomes altar, couch and chairs are the pews and grandson becomes Father as his nephew, Nicholas, helps him don the priestly vestments.

What a joy for all of us, but especially for my parents. The reading of the day echoed our reality, *"when every one of you shall return to his own property, every one to his family estate"* (Lev 251, 8-17), and the psalm asking that God *"let his face shine upon us"*. He truly did, and we saw and were so grateful.

Later we hiked down to the pristine little Crystal Lake for some swimming and canoeing, with the more adventuresome swinging on a rope and splashing into the cold water.

Paul Abraham is 35 today so a grand summer feast and the famous pie contest complete another memorable day.

Diary of a Country Carmelite

The earth has yielded its fruits:
God, our God has blessed us.
May God bless us
And may all the ends of the earth fear him.
(Psalm 67:7-8)

August 4, 2015

It is hard to find the time to live fully and also to write what has trans-
pired in the last few days. We have basked in all the rest and relaxation
that the little cabin in the Big Woods can provide and all the joys and
clamor of family togetherness. More paddles in the canoe, card games
and scrabble tournaments, cookouts and laughter; each day crowned
with Holy Mass. The small house overflows so a friend of Mom and
Dad's has lent us the use of her summer retreat. Andy and I and Fr.
Tom drive over each evening for the quiet and rest; sometimes with
Lauds and Vespers prayed together on the screen porch.

One day a local priest, Fr. Rendell, comes to lunch and we have
the joy of seeing again two young priests get to know each other and
share their mutual vision and vocation. That evening we advance Fr.
Tom's birthday by a few months and surprise him with a celebration.
We fit in as much as we can into his days at home.

This morning, the feast of St. John Vianney, the patron saint of
parish priests, we drive to Our Lady of Hope in Whitehall, NY for
a Holy Hour and rosary, then Fr. Tom concelebrates Holy Mass. He
proclaims the Gospel account of a storm rising on the Sea of Galilee,
the fearful fishermen, Christ seen approaching them, Peter's impetuous stepping out onto the waves ... his floundering.

Fr. Tom talks to us about his fun on the lake with his nieces and
nephew. No one walks *on* the water though. With Peter all is well as

138

long as his eyes are on Jesus. He becomes distracted and fearful ... as do we ... when we take our eyes and our trust off God. If only we could remember this when it is storming!

Mother introduces us to some ladies after Mass who have come to know our family and Tim through the *Diary of a Country Mother*, and I marvel again at how Tim keeps bringing people into our lives, with Grandma Six's help, of course.

After lunch we say our farewells, collect our paraphernalia and pile into our cars for the ride home. Fr. Tom and Paul have planned a stop on the way back at an ice cream stand and golf driving range. There's a lot of laughter and joking as the inexpert swingers try to connect with the ball. I play a hilarious game of miniature golf with Bella and Tiri, then it's back in the cars again.

As we head south, we watch the threatening clouds approach, followed by a brief rainstorm. And then, for over an hour, we drive towards a full double rainbow. As we near home I send up my prayers of thankfulness for all the beauty and bounty of our family, our world and our God.

> *Enter into his gates with thanksgiving.*
> *And into his courts with praise.* (Psalm 99:4)

August 5, 2015

Today is the feast of the Dedication of St. Mary Major, the oldest Roman Basilica dedicated to Mary. It was also the site of Fr. Tom's First Mass after his ordination, where, in a tiny subterranean chapel, there is displayed a relic of the true crib of Bethlehem.

We are on our way to the Visitation Monastery in Tyringham where Tom will offer Mass for the nuns. On the quiet drive I think about all the joys and sorrows that are the everyday reality in each of our lives. Today is a joy and I push aside the sorrow that this visit will have an end. How our time here on earth is a great longing for that family reunion that will have no end, no partings or good-byes.

Then the pure joy of being a participant in Holy Mass, the perfectly celebrated sacrifice by our own son. The Gospel we hear is from St. Matthew who tells of the persistent Canaanite woman who begs for the "table scraps" of a miracle for her daughter. Fr. Thomas asks the sisters … and all of us … if we pray with perseverance. Do we? Oh, that we could have Our Lord compliment us as He did the mother who wouldn't give up, "O woman, great is your faith! Let it be done for you as you wish!"

After Mass, the extern sister beckons us into a little room where a table has been set up for three. Andy and I and Fr. Tom are treated as royal guests with the breakfast that has been prepared for us. Another joy! The sisters have so thoughtfully provided for us, with beauty and simplicity, even as they prepare for Sr. Ann Margaret's funeral the next day. Joy and sorrow, but always full of love!

As we eat and sip our coffee and tea, Fr. Tom contrasts this morning, the well-laid out sacristy, perfectly appointed sanctuary, altar and music, with the Masses he celebrated in a string of towns and villages in Mexico during Holy Week. In one particular town, the people had been constructing a church, but it was unfinished and there was no electricity, so the Mass, offered after dark, was illuminated by two villagers holding flashlights on either side of the altar. What great faith and what a yearning for Christ to be among them!

I write a little note to the sisters before we head home and then we stop in the quiet chapel to give thanks to Him for the gift of this day, this life, this faith, this great love.

We head back home, but He lives within us, our Life, our Love, our Guest.

Within us there is a palace of immense magnificence. The entire edifice is built of gold and precious stones.... Truly there is no building of such great beauty as a pure soul, filled with virtues, and the greater these virtues, the brighter these stones sparkle.... In this palace the great King lodges, Who has been pleased to become your Guest, and ... He sits there on a throne of tremendous value: your heart. (St. Teresa of Avila, *Interior Castle*)

August 6, 2015

It's another beautiful day in Blandford, as only a midsummer day can be. Good news for Andy who has been waiting for Fr. Tom to come and help him with a few projects. Andy climbs a ladder to repair some leaks in the barn roof while Fr. Tom keeps a harness taut in case his dad slips. Then it's off to the lawn next to the vegetable garden to dig up some large rocks that are getting in the way of the mower. Fr. Tom comes up with some creative ways to move them and decides we should start a grotto behind the Mary garden with some of the rocks. Then he proceeds to make me a stone "seat" on top of the rock wall facing the little shrine to Mary. His thoughtfulness and artistic sense combine with this simple idea, which does entail a great deal of muscle to roll, lift and level the large boulder.

In the late afternoon we drive down the mountain and beside the river to St. Thomas Cemetery where we spend a few minutes sprucing up the little garden around Tim's grave stone. It's a good time to pray, too, in the quiet and kneeling in the posture of prayer. When all is tidy we bring a folding table and some chairs from the car, a crisp white tablecloth, a small arrangement of flowers, candles and Fr. Tom's Mass kit. Paul and Jasmine arrive with their three and help us set up the table, which will become our altar.

Diary of a Country Carmelite

It is the perfect day for a Mass in the cemetery—the Feast of the Transfiguration. Fr. Tom, still Tim's brother, dons the white vestments of the day and now, as priest, with Kateri assisting as altar server, pronounces the solemn words that bring us together. *"In the name of the Father, and of the Son, and of the Holy Spirit."* The Sign of the Cross.

On Mount Tabor, Christ, in the company of Moses and Elijah, revealed His glory and divinity to Peter, James and John, so after the scandal of the Cross they would remember and be heartened.

For our family it is a reminder that we are all striving for a glimpse of that glory and divinity, not just a momentary glimpse, but an eternity of the Beatific Vision, where we will actually get to build those three tents that Peter, so full of zeal, wished to set up. This Mass today is also a reminder for us that the family circle was not in reality broken with Tim's death. Tim's immortal soul *is* and someday will be joined to a remade, glorified body. He still loves us, prays for us and wants us to be with him again, too.

What then is to be done?

"Carry on!" ... "Soldier on!" ... Live in grace, die in grace. Love! Love! Love!

At the moment of consecration Christ is with our family in the little cemetery, feeling our pain, feeling our joy, tightening the circle.

After a while the other-worldly transcendence fades, but I still feel its pull. We quietly fold up the chairs, pack up the car and say our "good-byes", going back to our ordinary lives as did Peter, James and John.

Back home we find Andy's brother Jim has come to join us for dinner and as I pull the bread from the oven, stir the garden vegetables and chicken into the pasta and pour the iced tea, I think about the goodness of simple food, shared around a picnic table and smile to hear Tiri pipe up at the end of our grace, "Sacred Heart of Jesus" while with one voice we proclaim: "bring peace to our family." Amen!

August 7, 2015

I wake up early this morning to try and put the finishing stitches on a baby quilt I am hoping to deliver today to our nephew, Steve, the new father of Fulton Bonaventure. It's another fine summer morning and the quiet house and stillness outside settle a sense of peace over all as I snip the final threads.

This morning we are traveling to Pittsfield, about an hour away, for the funeral of Steve's grandfather, Eli William, the father of my sister-in-law, Gail. The route we take is mostly rural and brings us over Washington Mountain, a touch of beauty on this sober day. I have the quilt on my lap as we drive and am embroidering a small heart onto one corner so there can be a visible connection between the new baby and his great-grandfather.

At the funeral home, Fr. Tom is escorted to a small room where he begins to hear confessions, a particular request of a number of the grandchildren. We hand over the car keys to Fr. Tom after a while so our vehicle can be a mobile confessional on the way to church. Then, even though he has the necessary permission to concelebrate the Mass, Fr. Tom enters the confessional to be available for friends and relatives during the Mass.

There is a steady stream of "customers". Perhaps as a result of the prayers and sufferings of William who in his last days said, "I want to see all my family in heaven." Now that's the sort of legacy to leave behind, especially as that wish was preceded and followed by prayer.

In the Carmelite world, today is the feast of St. Albert of Trapani, a Carmelite priest who hailed from a town near Mount Trapani in Sicily. As the story goes, his parents were childless for 26 years but kept praying that they would be blessed with a child, even making a vow that any son or daughter conceived would be consecrated to Mary. Enter Albert!

One can only think that this dedication to Mary paid off royally. Albert entered the Carmelite monastery as a young man and his ordination to the priesthood was followed by his election as provincial of the Order. Even during his life he had a reputation for sanctity and miracles, as in the healing of a blind man and purifying the water in a well.

In 1282, history records, he served the sick and wounded during a revolt against the French regime and in the Siege of Messina he negotiated with the French to let provisions be brought into the city.

Albert's concerns for *his* people were for the whole person—body and soul. He lived in poverty, practiced a lively charity, excelled as an exorcist and showed a marked concern for the Jews.

Albert died on August 7, 1306, and though never formally canonized, his feast was introduced in the 15th century. St. Teresa of Avila called him "one of the holy protectors of the Order".

What will be said of each of us after we die? Today's funeral and its Carmelite feast remind us that this life is empty without a spiritual legacy … without a life intent on a belief in God, on good works and on Love.

May the great Communion of Saints, our everyday, simple heroes and those canonized "by the book" bolster our resolve to keep on struggling and to make each moment a total response to grace.

August 9, 2015

Andy and I are in the car, driving back home on the Massachusetts Turnpike after delivering Fr. Tom to Logan Airport in Boston. The ride normally takes several hours, barring any significant traffic, so

I have time to rest, remember and pray as Andy manfully shoulders the driving.

Yesterday was a lovely final day for all of us, beginning with a Mass for family and friends at our parish. How often is it that a grandfather gets to serve Mass when his grandson is the celebrant and a father to read such words from Deuteronomy?

> Hear, O Israel! The Lord is our God, the Lord alone! There-fore, you shall love the Lord, your God, with all your heart, and with all your soul, and with all your strength. Take to heart these words which I enjoin on you today. Drill them into your children. Speak of them at home or abroad, whether you are busy or at rest. (Deut 6:4-7)

Yes, Lord, we did and now, this child of ours is serving and loving You with all his heart. More prayers of gratitude!

At home we worked and played, baked pies with the grandchildren and enjoyed our "last supper" together, for the time being anyway.

Then, this morning, with Fr. Tom's suitcases stowed away in the back of the car, we left for an early Mass at St. Mary's in Westfield followed by a family breakfast at a small restaurant around the corner. What fun we had as the syrup was passed around after grace. We even managed to fit in a last romp in the park and a family photo.

On the ride to the airport, we heard the homily Fr. Tom would have given if the concelebrating priest had asked him. The Gospel from John was one of the "Bread of Life" discourses. Jesus firmly declares to the murmuring Jews, "*I am the Bread of Life … .the living bread that came down from heaven; whoever eats this bread will live forever, and the bread that I will give is my flesh for the life of the world.*"

Do we have the strength to get to heaven? At every Mass and at every Eucharist we have the chance, Fr. Tom said, for a heart tissue transplant … to receive the heart of Christ, our "strength for the journey".

Diary of a Country Carmelite

How perfect! Our own private homily as we headed east toward the airport. We prayed the Office of Readings together en-route and savored the last minutes of our son's company. Good-byes are always bittersweet, but particularly when you are not sure when you will see each other again. Our next visit could be several years away.

As we drove up to the airport and stopped to unload the luggage, we received not only Fr. Tom's embrace, but also his priestly blessing—a great comfort for us. Then he "gave" each of us a saint for the year. For Dad, St. Thomas More, quite fitting for his father the town selectman. My saint, a dear familiar figure, just happened to be St. Teresa Benedicta of the Cross, or as she is also known, Edith Stein.

Of course, Fr. Tom knew that today was her feast day and that she was a Carmelite nun, so it was also most appropriate for me.

St. Teresa Benedicta is well known in Catholic circles and beyond and her story is quite dramatic and inspiring, especially now in this time and age. Born of Jewish parents in Germany in 1891, she grew up in a very devout, observant Jewish family. As a young one, her older brothers and sisters made a point of showing off their little sister's amazing intelligence and memory. Over the years that followed, study became her most compelling interest, with philosophy, psychology, history and German literature becoming the areas of her expertise and most concentrated endeavor.

Beginning with a superficial Jewish faith, then moving on to atheism, Edith was always on the hunt for "truth". This huntress, now so serious to find her prey, began to study phenomenology with the Christian philosopher Edmund Husserl. And she felt she was getting close. With her mind well-tuned by her study and her life intertwined with some serious Christians, Edith happened upon a copy of the autobiography of St. Teresa of Avila. Reading all night through, by morning she was convinced that she had found truth and was on the path to becoming a Catholic.

As we read about the details of a person's life, the people God sends and the circumstances that appear to be random, it all seems so dramatic and amazing! How wonderful God is in His watchfulness.

Edith sought Baptism in 1922 and then followed more study, teaching and lecturing, all interspersed with attempts to explain her actions to her family and trying to discern a call to the religious life. There were many trials along the way as she saw her widowed mother's pain and as she watched the rise of Nazi ideology in her land. Edith recognized the suffering of the Jews as her suffering too, and embraced this call to suffer with them as she embraced her vocation to Carmel. She entered the Cologne Carmel in 1933 and there followed a few peaceful years. By 1942 she was living in a Carmelite convent in Echt, Netherlands, which her superiors thought would be a safer place than Germany. With the invasion of Holland by the Nazis, there was no safety for Edith and her sister Rosa, who was now a Catholic as well and living with her. In 1942 they were both arrested by the Gestapo and whisked off to a series of concentration camps, with Auschwitz being their final destination and the site of their holocaust. Edith had known the cross and as Sr. Benedicta of the Cross had embraced the suffering she knew was inevitable, offering her life finally on behalf of her Jewish family—on behalf of all Jews.

I think of the two sisters, Edith and Rosa, walking hand in hand toward the gas chamber, their human emotions overlaid by the strength of their act of heroism.

The giving up of my son on the curb of the airport is a small gesture compared to their martyrdom, but it is nonetheless the little gift I am asked to make today. I do it cheerfully, arm in arm with Andy, but with the strong hands of Edith and Rosa on my shoulders.

We will meet again on the great day,
The day of manifest glory,
When above the head of the Queen of Carmel

Diary of a Country Carmelite

The crown of stars will gleam brilliantly,
Because the twelve tribes will have found their Lord."
(Teresa Benedicta of the Cross, *Conversation at Night*, a
play about Queen Esther)

August 15, 2015

I wake this morning before 4 and decide to get up and use the early
morning quiet and stillness to tidy up the house a bit. I fold some
sheets and pillowcases and put the guest bedrooms back in order after
the company of the past weeks. I fold the small white tablecloth we
had used on the "altar" and slip it into a drawer until it is needed again.

When I sit down and compose myself for mental prayer the sky
is beginning to lighten and the crows are raising a ruckus. I pull out
Divine Intimacy and open up to the back pages of feasts. There it is:
The Assumption of the Blessed Virgin Mary.

Fr. Gabriel reminds us that in pondering Mary's assumption into
heaven we contemplate the reality *"that our permanent abode is not on
earth but in heaven where she, with her divine Son, has preceded us in the fullness
of her human nature,"* and *"It is a reminder to us to ennoble our whole life, not
only that of the spirit, but also that of the senses, elevating it to the heights of the
celestial life which awaits us."* What good, substantial food for meditation!

The morning continues with Lauds, prayed alone and silently today,
and then I carry all these thoughts outside into the beauty of a new
summer morning as I un-coop the chickens, fill their feeder and water
the plants. How I love the quiet morning in the garden!

Paul is working this morning so we pick up the grandchildren for
Mass, enjoying our conversations in the car about just what we are
celebrating on this holy day. The word "assumption" does have other
meanings, of course, and we clear up any misconceptions.

Then up the steps and into the church for the great feast of heaven and earth, joining us with our Creator and Redeemer and the Spirit of their Love and with Mary, Mother of us all. Under her mantle, too, a host of unseen souls, our Tim among them, who have all earned that blessed rest.

Later in the evening, the clouds move in and we are treated to lightning, thunder and pouring rain. While I am grateful for this watering of all the fruits, vegetables and flowers, it brings to mind our great dependence on the providence of God for the fruitfulness of all we attempt, both in the physical realm and in the spiritual. With prayers to our Mother who has gone before us, may we so ennoble every action, thought and prayer that, like her, we reach the "*heights of celestial life which await us*".

August 16, 2015

After Mass and a quiet afternoon in the shade, Paul and the children come by on their way home from a hike. We cook and wash up together, then enjoy ice cream cones at the picnic table outside. Later we drive down the mountain for a fireworks display at Stanley Park, which had been rained out last month.

As we sit and play on a great expanse of lawn with a host of other families doing the same, the sky darkens and the stars pop out. The first burst of sound and light signals the opening of the entertainment. What beauty has been provided for us! With Kateri on my lap, pressing her hands over her ears, I sit in the present moment and enjoy the scene.

The mind wanders a bit and I ponder a time in the 1930s in Spain when freedom of any sort was in short supply. Today's Carmelite holy one, celebrated when the 16th doesn't fall on a Sunday, lived and suffered in those dark days in Toledo.

Diary of a Country Carmelite

Born in 1881, Elvira Moragas Cantarero already stood out, even before her death in August of 1936. A woman pharmacist in an age when only men held this position, Elvira should have been content with practicing this well-respected profession, as had her father before her. But she felt the call of a higher way of life and entered the Carmel of St. Anne and St. Joseph in 1915. Now she was known as Sr. Maria Sagrario of St. Aloysius Gonzaga and excelled here as well, with her love of the Eucharist and her penchant for the contemplative life. She was elected prioress in 1927 and novice mistress in 1930. Testimonies indicated that she told her novices that she desired martyrdom. All seemed to fall into place for this desire to become a reality.

First, Blessed Maria was again elected prioress in 1936, two weeks before the beginning of the Spanish Civil War broke out. The convent was rushed by an angry mob, but the prioress, keeping her head under pressure, managed to get her sisters to safety. She and another nun found refuge in the home of her fellow sister's family. They were discovered the next day and arrested. Not even this disturbed Sr. Maria Sagrario's calm, though. She was interrogated and treated roughly but did not give away the whereabouts of the rest of the nuns. The following day, the feast of the Assumption, she was executed. Her fellow Carmelites survived this time of terror, thanks to her protection, and she gave a strong witness to the Spanish people of her faith in Christ and His Church.

What a display of fireworks we should have in her honor!

May Jesus reign always in my heart. The Lord asks me to be humble, to weep over my sins, to love him much, to love my sisters much, to mortify them in nothing, not to mortify myself uselessly, to live recollected in him wanting nothing for myself, completely surrendered to his divine will.

In this vale of tears, suffering will not be lacking and we should be content to have something to offer to our most beloved Jesus who wanted so much to suffer for love of us.

The most direct way to unite ourselves to God is that of the cross, so we should always desire it. May the Lord not permit that I be separated from his divine will. (Blessed Maria Sagrario, *Letters and Writings*)

August 18, 2015

Another summer day in the hills, another day of beauty in the height of the growing season. It all seems so timeless, but reason and experience tell me that the blooms and fruits won't last forever. I drive down into Westfield for morning Mass, admiring other gardens as I pass by them. It's always a good image for the spiritual life, too. Working in the garden is good, but how much more productive to be cultivating fruits that will never fade?

The Gospel this morning provides more food for contemplation. I think about that rich man and the impossibility of the camel going through the gate that is called the "Eye of the Needle". Do I have that actual spirit of poverty that Jesus is calling us, calling *me*, to replicate in my life?

Later, when I pray the Office of Readings for today's saints, I read the *Resolution* that a group of priests, imprisoned on the French ship, *Les Deux Associes*, drew up to encourage one another. I wonder if my spirit of poverty could *ever* be equal to theirs.

If God permits them to recover totally or in part this liberty nature longs for, they will avoid giving themselves up to immoderate joy when they receive the news. By keeping their souls tranquil, they will show they support without murmur the cross placed on them and that they are disposed to bear it even longer with courage and as true Christians who never let themselves be beaten by adversity.

Diary of a Country Carmelite

Three Carmelite priests, Fr. John-Baptiste Duverneuil, Fr. Michel-Louis Brulard and Fr. Jacques Gagnot, were among the 64 imprisoned, all caught up in the anti-Catholic fury of the Revolution in France.

It is a good thing for us to look at each one individually, to understand his life and the circumstances God permitted for him to make this ultimate sacrifice.

Fr. Jean-Baptiste Duverneuil was born in Limoges in 1759 and first entered the seminary where he was ordained in 1780, only later joining the Discalced Carmelite Order, where he was given the name Fr. Leonard. He spent some time in the community in Angouleme until the suppression of religious orders when he traveled back to Limoges. He remained faithful to the Catholic Church and refused any compliance with the new regime. As a result, he was arrested in 1794 and condemned to deportation to French Guiana. None of our three priests ever reached Guiana, though, as conditions on board the slave traders were so horrific.

Fr. Leonard did not give up his life of prayer, but with the other priests and religious on board, recited the prayers of the Mass together, prayed the psalms, tended the sick and anointed the dying. Fr. Leonard himself moved into the ranks of the suffering and finally died on board ship, sick and wasted away, on July 1, 1794. He was just 35 years old.

His fellow Carmelite, Fr. Michel-Louis Brulard was born in Chartres in 1758. He studied theology at Paris University, then after finishing, entered the Carmelite Order at the monastery in Charenton. He also was forced to return to his home in Chartres, and like Fr. Leonard was arrested when he refused to deny his faith and allegiance to Rome. Fr. Michel-Louis received a similar sentence and died a similar death. He was just 36 years old. One of his fellow prisoners attested: "*One could never believe, without having been a witness, that a living body could reach such an inconceivable stage of emaciation to which I saw him reduced*" but also that he "*spoke no other language except that of the purest spirituality*".

Our third Blessed, Fr. Jacques Gagnot, hailed from Frolois and made his religious profession at the Carmelite monastery in Nancy in 1774. He served at the monastery in Lunenville but was back in Nancy when the time of the dissolution of religious orders was commanded. Leaving to find refuge with a family in the town, he was finally denounced as a "perilous fanatic" and sentenced to deportation in 1794. He was able to write his mother, though, who must have so treasured his letter after his death.

> It is true that when one considers all this with the eyes of the world, there is nothing but dread, now that, in effect, one is tossed out of one's country, not knowing what will happen, exposed to hunger, thirst, without clothing, in a word, a thousand deaths, I have the fortune that awaits us. However, seen from the eyes of faith, considering that the Lord has found us worthy of suffering for his holy name, that we are persecuted in the name of the faith, all this encourages and stimulates us with holy zeal to defend the Roman, apostolic, Catholic religion in which we were born and in which we hope to die…! How many Saints before us have been exiled! It is truly a grace that the Lord is giving us…. We have to trust him, and since he has given us the grace to begin well, we will always ask him the grace of perseverance.

Fr. Gagnot *was* given the grace of perseverance and, after tending the sick among his fellow priests and religious, died himself on Septemeber 10, 1794, at the age of 41.

What a lesson these three martyrs have to teach us; a lesson that is as timeless now as it was then. In the words of Fr. Camilo Maccise, OCD, the Superior General in 1995, when the priests were beatified:

> Our brothers together with their fellow prisoners, chose to lose privileges, goods, opportunities for the future instead

of breaking with Rome and the Pope, the bond of unity and communion between all believers. In this way they testified to that, which we today call a Church of communion, which has its origin in Christ and which continues on in the Petrine ministry.

In doing this our three brothers gave witness to the proverbial love for the Church of our holy Mother Teresa. A love which led her to renew Carmel in an era of division stemming from the Protestant reform. (*Faithful to God and the Church*, Circular Letter to the Order)

May each of us possess that love and show it to the world in any difficulties we may encounter in this life.

August 22, 2015

This year the feast of the Queenship of Mary falls on the fourth Saturday of the month, so our little Carmelite community is together for Mass in Turners Falls. Then we have the joy of praying Lauds together at the conclusion of Mass. Instead of moving downstairs to the undercroft for our meeting, though, we get back in our cars and drive over the border into Vermont.

A few years ago, we accepted the invitation of Pete and Judith, our husband and wife Carmelites, to spend one Saturday a year availing ourselves of their great hospitality. We each bring something to contribute to the feast, but Pete's homemade wine and Judith's Italian dishes are the stars of the show. We take some time, amid forkfuls and sips, to engage in the conversations that help us get to know our "family" better and to strengthen the familial bonds. We hear about family milestones, tuck prayer intentions away in our memories and relax for a few hours. Deacon George tells us about a homily he gave, not too long ago, about the human heart. We sit "at his feet" and listen and I think about Mary's queenly heart.

We venerate her as Queen and Mother, but it is the heart of Mary that prompts all her aid to those of us still toiling here below. In the Office of Readings, St. Amadeus of Lausanne lays it out beautifully:

> Dwelling in the loftiest citadel of virtue, like a sea of divine grace or an unfathomable source of love that has everywhere overflowed its banks, she poured forth her bountiful waters on trusting and thirsting souls. Able to preserve both flesh and spirit from death she bestowed health-giving salve on bodies and souls. Has anyone ever come away from her troubled or saddened or ignorant of the heavenly mysteries? Who has not returned to everyday life gladdened and joyful because his request had been granted by the Mother of God?

At the end of the day, we pack up, offer our thanks and say our good-byes, "gladdened and joyful" after a morning honoring Mary and an afternoon spent together in her presence. What a lovely foretaste of heavenly joy. Deo Gratias!

August 25, 2015

I had planned to head out to the garden early this morning, but the rain keeps me inside for now. Sadly, I am not one of those die-hard gardeners who work in *any* kind of weather. The fall lettuce will get planted another day, God willing!

There is plenty to do inside, as always. I fold the laundry, then work for a while on piecing a baby quilt for a new grandnephew. It is a task made pleasant by the joy in seeing the pattern take shape as I cut and sew the squares and strips.

Diary of a Country Carmelite

During Lauds this morning I prayed the Office of Readings of today's Carmelite saint and thought again with amazement about her life and the glaringly obvious presence of God in the circumstances that preceded her birth and followed her along the way.

Mariam Baouardy was born near Nazareth in 1846, but her story begins long before that. Her mother had given birth to twelve sons but all had died in infancy.

Being the devout Catholics that they were, her parents traveled to Bethlehem on pilgrimage to the Grotto of the Nativity, begging God to give them the joy of children.

So, little Mariam was, first and foremost, a child born of the fervent prayer of her parents. A little brother followed but the intact family was not to remain so for very long. Both her parents died when Mariam was two. Her brother went to live with her mother's sister and she with her father's brother. The two little ones were never to see each other again in this life.

Mariam was loved by her aunt and uncle during her childhood, but this little one, dedicated by her parents to the Virgin Mary at her birth, was marked for particular sufferings and given mystical gifts. From the age of five she fasted on Saturdays in honor of Mary and was devout in the practice of her faith. She also had angelic visitors in times of crisis and heard voices that gave her direction when there was no one else to help.

In her teens, life took a turn for the worse when she refused a marriage her uncle had arranged. He beat her in his rage and, when this did not have any effect, treated her as the lowliest servant. A Muslim in the household offered to help her but she soon found out he wanted to marry her and force her conversion to Islam. Resisting him, she was again the target of another's anger as he slit her throat and left her for dead in an alley. The poor motherless child was tended by a "lady in blue", none other than Mary of Nazareth. (You really must read this story in all its detail!)

Once she recovered, Mariam worked as a household servant in several places and eventually entered the Carmelites in France, helped to begin a community in India and finally went "home" to found a Carmel in Bethlehem and to plan for one in Nazareth. Now known as St. Mary of Jesus Crucified, she was canonized this year by Pope Francis in May, exemplifying the joy of a true follower of Christ and also the suffering. She bore the stigmata and endured serious persecution in her short life.

The "Little Arab", humble in stature as well as in her poverty of spirit, was gifted by God with a host of mystical phenomena besides the stigmata: bilocation, levitation and ecstasies to name a few. She died in 1878 at the age of 33 but lives on in her heavenly homeland as well as in the hearts and memories of all the Carmelites and Middle Eastern Catholics who hold her dear.

How different is my life from hers! I live on the other side of the world, in a country of privilege, have parents who are still alive in their 80s and have the work of a wife and mother.

Despite this, I claim her as my sister in Carmel and feel a strong affinity to this little nun. The saints among us are both timeless and universal after all. They love us with an everlasting charity and one day we will come to know just how much each one has contributed to making certain that we join them in the great family reunion under the gaze of the Trinity.

> The whole world is asleep, and God so full of goodness, so great, so worthy of all praise, and hardly no one is thinking of Him! See, nature praises Him, the sky, the stars, the trees, the grass, everything praises Him, and man, who has knowledge of His benefits, who ought to praise Him, sleeps! Let us go, let us go and wake up the universe! (St. Mary of Jesus Crucified)

Diary of a Country Carmelite

August 26, 2015

As I was making Andy's lunch this morning, I mentioned that it was the feast of the Transverberation of St. Teresa. Raised eyebrows and a puzzled look were his response. It's not a common word and it doesn't appear in our 1,149-page dictionary.

I explained briefly that we were celebrating an event in the life of St. Teresa when a small, beautiful angel of light or cherubim plunged a fiery dart several times into her heart causing not only great physical and spiritual pain but also a sweetness which left her "all on fire with great love of God".

> This is the fire the Lord Himself came to cast upon the earth.
> It is the fire flaming forth from the furnace of mystical communion. (Thomas Dubay, S.M., *Fire Within*)

Many writers have noted that the founders of religious congregations that will have a great influence on the world have been the recipients of extraordinary, divine gifts that not only are beneficial to them individually, but to all their "spiritual children".

This great love of God is diffusive in its essence and meant to be shared with those God places in our lives.

Very sublime thoughts for a country housewife sending her man off to work with his lunch!

After Mass this morning I bring my granddaughters Bella and Tiri back to the hills where we are playing at being pioneers from another century. They wear aprons over their dresses, we bake bread, work in the garden weeding and picking vegetables, make patchwork pillows and for dinner "farm soup" to go with our bread.

How easy and delightful it is … some days … to show God's love!

AUGUST

Almighty God, you filled the heart of St. Teresa of Avila our Mother with the fire of your love and you gave her strength to undertake difficult tasks for the honor of your name. Through her prayers may the power of your love fill our hearts also and stir us to ever more generous efforts in your service. We ask this through our Lord Jesus Christ, your Son who lives and reigns with you and the Holy Spirit, one God forever and ever. Amen.

September

September 1, 2015

Another still, crisp morning. Summer is winding down and I sit on the porch with my cup of tea to savor the beauty for a few minutes. Later, I make my way outside for a little work in the garden, watering the flower pots, checking the leaves for Japanese beetles and giving the vegetables a once-over to see what needs picking today. Then, with all the preliminary work behind me, I get to the real business of the morning—mowing on the garden tractor—which really *is* my vehicle for meditation.

I steer around the flower and berry beds, around the little Japanese maple and rugosa rose hedge and then around and around, back and forth on the long swaths of grass, the rhythm and repetition stilling my active, conscious mind and once again ushering me into a deeper stillness.

I think about today's saint, Teresa Margaret Redi, and my attraction to her. A year or so ago I read *From the Sacred Heart to the Trinity: The Spiritual Itinerary of St. Teresa Margret (Redi) of the Sacred Heart, O.C.D.,* by Fr. Gabriel of St. Mary Magdalene, OCD, and was drawn in to a profound appreciation for this little Tuscan Carmelite whose life spanned a few short decades in the 18th century.

After I read the book, I wrote about Teresa Margaret for our community newsletter and then a month later gathered a group of women onto the porch for a discussion of her life and spirituality. How delightful to be able to share a friend that I had never met with my own dear ones.

St. Teresa Margaret Marianne of the Sacred Heart was born Anna Maria Redi in Arezzo, Italy on July 15, 1747, the second of thirteen children. From all accounts she was a serious child who recognized early on that God was the one thing most important and she sought for ways to prove her love to Him. That doesn't mean that she had no faults, however. She was the little helper to her mother in caring for her brothers and sisters, who noted that she had a fiery temperament and at times would resort to force in order to keep them in line.

Anna Maria was very close to her father, Ignatius, and she benefitted in many ways from this familial relationship. Her father introduced her to the devotion to the Sacred Heart of Jesus and drew her often into conversation in the evenings to discuss the life of faith. Hers was the ideal Catholic family, where daily Mass and family prayer were the norm. Orchards and gardens made up the family lands and Anna Maria loved the solitude and beauty they afforded, while keeping busy at work in them.

She entered a Benedictine boarding school in Florence at the age of nine and loved the sisters there, growing quickly in the life of virtue and prayer. In fact, she thought seriously about entering the Benedictine order until a chance encounter at a friend's parting to join the Carmelites turned her in another direction. Twice she heard a voice which identified itself as *"Teresa of Jesus"* and told her she would be numbered among Teresa's daughters. This experience moved Anna Maria greatly and she pondered it in silence before seeking the approval of her parents and several priests who were adept at discerning vocations.

Thus, we see the saint entering the Carmel of Florence at the age of seventeen to realize the dream of her life: to love God and so attempt to return in some small way the love that had been showered upon her. Parting from her family was a painful affair for her but she recognized the need for a heroic detachment, especially in regard to the relationship with her father. She was emotionally distraught and knew the cost of this huge sacrifice but promised her father to greet him each night in the Sacred Heart of Jesus.

Convent life was the garden where Anna Maria, now Teresa Margaret of the Sacred Heart, bloomed, but also where she found the most painful thorns. Acting to assist the infirmarian, and later holding that post herself, she gave of her time and energies without reserve and struggled mightily to overcome the strong repugnance she felt in dealing with some difficult personalities, especially one of her charges, who had slipped into a severe mental illness.

> Knowing that a bride cannot be pleasing to her spouse unless she endeavors to become what he wishes her to be ... I will always think of my neighbors as beings made in your likeness, produced by your divine love, redeemed at the price of your precious Blood, looking upon them with true Christian charity, which you command. I will sympathize with their troubles, excuse their faults, always speak well of them, and never willingly fail in charity towards them in thought, word, or deed. (St. Teresa Margaret of the Sacred Heart of Jesus)

All the while, the depth of her spiritual life was growing as she sought only to please God and to do His will, to mortify her own will and to put her whole intellectual life in the hands of God. She strove to remain in the Eucharistic presence of Christ throughout the day and to maintain a harmony between her active duties and her life of prayer. Her devotion to the Sacred Heart deepened as well and she received permission from her confessor to use a biography of Margaret Mary Alacoque as her model and inspiration, going so far as to call her "my mistress" in learning and applying the love of the Sacred Heart.

Diary of a Country Carmelite

In 1767 while assisting at the recitation of the Divine Office, Teresa Margaret was overwhelmed with a mystical grace at hearing the words, "God is love". This thought, which had been so familiar to her, was internally personified and it threw her into an absorption with God which marked the rest of her earthly life. We hear from her confessor, Fr. Idlephonse:

> She told me about divine things, remarking that this charity is the same love with which God loves Himself from all eternity, the Spirit of God Himself, Which is His life and His breath, Who is the Holy Spirit, the Third Person of the Blessed Trinity. And when it is said that he who dwells in charity dwells in God and God in him, the meaning is that he lives in the life of God and God, after a certain fashion, lives His life in him.

In the days and months that followed she sought to repay this love and found herself coming up painfully short, an experience which caused immense suffering in Teresa Margaret. She desired, like Thérèse, to be a victim of love, and like Thérèse, this was the cause of an overwhelming suffering. She desired to enter into the hidden life of Christ, the life of His intellectual suffering, and thus of His union with the Trinity.

Here we see the saint struggling with a severe mental and physical aridity, during which she tried to remain faithful to all her duties, bestowing her heightened charity upon her sick sisters and offering her powers of intercessory prayer at the service of the Church and the world. Her martyrdom had begun in earnest. She complained of a "dark soul" and "little courage" but kept manfully on the path of duty and love. All the while, her demeanor remained as it always had, one of cheerfulness and joy. After five years in Carmel at the age of twenty-two, a sudden illness quickly brought her to the point of death, without her sisters realizing the severity of the situation. Teresa Margaret was ever the model for the hidden life.

According to two of her confessors, she could not have remained alive much longer as, even without a bodily illness, she was on the verge of dying of love.

After death her body gradually lost the disfigurement of her illness and a beautiful fragrance emanated from her remains. Miracles began to be attributed to her intercession without delay. Today her incorrupt body lies in the Carmel of Florence, Italy.

I encourage you to pick up Fr. Gabriel's slim volume and then to read Edith Stein's chapter on our little saint from her book, *The Hidden Life*. Get to know our family's apostle of the Sacred Heart and the Trinity and sit at her feet for a while. You won't be sorry you did.

> Completely absorbed in Jesus and the beauties of His soul, Teresa Margaret desired only one thing: to participate in His love: to participate in His knowledge that plunged His intellect in to the mystery of the Trinity. (Fr. Gabriel of St. Mary Magdalene, OCD, *From the Sacred Heart to the Trinity*)

September 8, 2015

The past several days have been hot and humid, so I am grateful for the coolness this morning. I leave the house around 7:00 and relax in the quiet morning drive on my way to Mass at the Visitation Monastery in Tyringham. It's a peaceful drive on two-lane country roads and in the half-hour ride today, I don't think I passed even one car or truck. No traffic or anxiety on this route!

Instead, I catch a glimpse of several lakes and ponds, a swamp or two and the play of sunlight and shadow over the roads as I travel along. I can already see signs of the change of seasons. The ferns are turning brown and brittle, a few trees have yellow or orange leaves and the goldenrod, with its yellow, arched plumes, is everywhere in the fields and on the roadsides.

As I turn and head north, getting close to the monastery, the sun is high enough to shine brightly over the tops of the hills and it illumines all with clarity and vigor.

What a beauty of a day for this feast of the Nativity of Mary!

The nuns have a line-up of perfect Marian hymns, the priest, Fr. Sean, has a reverent manner and preaching style that both instructs and edifies with joy. God is good!

I am immensely grateful to have the time to be here today. I draw out my thanksgiving after Communion, to the music of flutes; no hurrying or rushing about this morning. I even have time to stay and pray the Office of Readings. With St. Andrew of Crete to bear me company, I read:

> Justly then do we celebrate this mystery since it signifies for us a double grace. We are led toward the truth, and we are led away from our condition of slavery to the letter of the law. How can this be? Darkness yields before the coming of light, and grace exchanges legalism for freedom. But midway between the two stands today's mystery, at the frontier where types and symbols give way to reality, and the old is replaced by the new.
>
> Therefore, let all creation sing and dance and unite to make worthy contribution to the celebration of this day. Let there be one common festival for saints in heaven and men on earth. Let everything, mundane things and those above, join in festive celebration. Today this created world is raised to the dignity of a holy place for him who made all things. The creature is newly prepared to be a divine dwelling place for the Creator.

Singing and dancing all the way home!

September 12, 2015

Today ends up being a day like a lot of other days. My "to do" list gets rearranged a little by a call for help. It is a joyful detour, though, as Kateri joins me on the ride home after Mass. Later on, we go to my friend Eileen's house to help her get ready for a birthday party. It can be difficult to put things in order and prepare food when you are hobbling about on crutches.

Back at home, we maneuver the tractor out of the barn and Tiri hops on my lap to practice her steering. Through all the activities of the morning I do my best, sometimes successfully, sometimes not, to place myself in the joy of the present moment and to work in the knowledge of the presence of God. Worry about the next task or the pile that awaits me only gets in the way of the serenity that is the prerequisite for prayer. A lesson that must be continually learned!

Today, I have the help of Blessed Mary of Jesus, a contemporary of our Holy Mother, St. Teresa. I do love the research that brings me to a deeper understanding of our Carmelite saints, discovering their *real* lives, struggles and personalities.

From all accounts, Mary Lopez Rivas was drawn to God even as a little child, constructing tiny churches in her play and dressing her dolls to resemble Our Lady. She also suffered many early trials—the death of her father and a move to live with her grandparents. It was here, though, that she came into contact with some holy Jesuits. Sickness plagued her, too, perhaps to remove her from the fracas of ordinary life so she would be able to hear Jesus and Mary directing her to Carmel.

She obeyed promptly and was recognized by Teresa as a soul of particular beauty. Except for Teresa's direct intervention, Sr. Mary of Jesus would have been dismissed from the Toledo convent for her poor health.

Diary of a Country Carmelite

Think well about what you are doing, because if you do not admit Sister Mary of Jesus to profession, I shall have her come to Avila; and the monastery that will have her will be the most fortunate of all. On my part, I would like to have her always with me in my monastery, even if she had to stay in bed all her life. (St. Teresa of Avial, *Letters*)

Teresa often went to consult her "letradillo" or little theologian, who at 23 became mistress of novices and later sub-prioress and prioress.

Mary recognized the role of suffering in this life, but she went further than that and prayed for suffering to come to her. It came in the form of physical pain—she endured the agony of an invisible crown of thorns and the piercing and throbbing in her hands and feet as if there were nails being driven into them. Perhaps more difficult to bear though, were the trials in Carmel. She was opposed by the nuns, falsely accused and later removed as prioress.

Through it all, Blessed Mary maintained a patient calm, promising Jesus never to pass a day without suffering given as gift. She was devoted to the Eucharist, seeing the Sacred Heart of her Lord present there, and often spoke about the importance of resting in union with Jesus.

To the Heart of my Jesus we have to fly as doves, and there, too, make our nest. (Blessed Mary of Jesus)

Despite the times of opposition within her community, she came to be regarded as a saint, even while living, and in death her sanctity became palpable, her body giving off a sweet fragrance and a scented oil.

Today her incorrupt body lies in Spain at the Toledo Carmel, and I invoke her intercession as she lives and breathes before the throne of the God whom she loved and served.

Blessed Mary of Jesus, make my heart like unto thine!

September 15, 2015

I made sure the house was clean and straightened this morning and then brewed a jar of sun tea and baked a chocolate mousse, placing it to chill in the freezer. With the house chores behind me I took some time to putter around outside, deadheading some flowers and giving the garden a once-over to make certain the flower beds were presentable and the vegetable plots not too riotous.

The Garden Club ladies are coming by tonight for a tour and my afternoon shift at the library doesn't end until 6, so there won't be time later to do any of this. I do make sure, though, that I stop in time to get to noon Mass before heading to work on this feast of Our Lady of Sorrows.

Yesterday we celebrated the Triumph of the Cross with more of an Easter joy than a Good Friday despondency. Today, however, we immerse ourselves in the soul and psyche of Mary as we contemplate her long martyrdom, beginning with the prophecy of Simeon, along all the years of her Son's hidden life and public ministry and on to the intensity of those last days, with Mary aware of the agony, pain, betrayal and suffering up the path to the hill of Calvary. "What sorrow can compare with my sorrow?"

Before Mass I sit and pray the Office of Readings and let St. Bernard enlighten me.

> Truly, O Blessed Mother, a sword has pierced your heart. For only by passing through your heart could the sword enter the flesh of your Son. Indeed, after your Jesus—who belongs to everyone, but is especially yours—gave up his life, the cruel spear, which was not withheld from his lifeless body, tore open his side. Clearly it did not touch his soul and could not

harm him, but it did pierce your heart. For surely his soul was no longer there, but yours could not be torn away. Thus the violence of sorrow has cut through your heart, and we rightly call you more than martyr, since the effect of compassion in you has gone beyond the endurance of physical suffering.... He died in body through a love greater than anyone had known. She died in spirit through a love unlike any other since his. (St. Bernard, Abbot, *Sermon,* Office of Readings, Our Lady of Sorrows)

As I show the ladies around in the evening, we come to the Mary Garden—her little place of honor in all the beauty of her Son's design. The statue in its rustic, wooden shrine depicts the young Mother with infant pressed to her cheek. Perhaps she is pondering the words of Simeon, but also giving her "yes" to God with every breath and thought. I give her my nod of acknowledgement as I pass by and then it's on to the porch with a trail of gardeners behind me to toast her with a glass of iced tea and a spoon of dark chocolate.

May I, with Mary's help, remain faithful to the end to the promises I have made as her daughter in Carmel and never waver as I go through my own suffering.

Holy Mary, Mother of God, pray for us sinners now and at the hour of our death, Amen.

September 17, 2015

It has been a busy day today, rushing about from one thing to another. Straighten the house, feed the chickens, drive to Mass, then on to the library and, in the late afternoon, deliver a welcome basket to our newest town resident.

Once I am home for good, I take a stack of books and a glass of iced tea into a shady part of the yard to sit and "collect" myself for a while before heading in to make dinner.

It is so lovely and still here on the edge of the woods. After Evening Prayer, I sit in the silence for a bit and just listen. I hear a lawnmower, and a bit further away, a hay baler thumping ... someone chopping wood ... an assortment of birdsong. The breeze picks up for a minute and the light and shadows play around and over me.

All at once, in the stillness, I remember a portion from today's Office of Readings for the Feast of St. Albert of Jerusalem.

The Apostle would have us keep silence, for in silence he tells us to work. As the prophet also makes known to us, silence is the way to foster holiness. Elsewhere, he says, your strength will lie in silence and hope. (St. Albert of Jerusalem, from the *Rule* delivered to the Brothers of Mount Carmel)

What excellent advice and how seldom I take full advantage of it! I can remember as a busy mom how much I craved silence. And now that I can be immersed in it for great lengths of time, how often I prefer to turn on the radio or listen to an audio book or a podcast. Mea culpa!

But who was Albert of Jerusalem and why do Carmelites honor an Augustinian with a Feast?

Albert of Avogadro, an Italian by birth, was born in the mid-12th century, a time of turmoil on many fronts. Happily, though, it was also an era in which both the culture bloomed and religious life saw some much-needed reforms.

Albert, the astute lawyer, the theologian and peacemaker, the prayerful man who was also full of common sense, had his part to play in the drama. Some years after his priestly ordination he was elected prior of his Augustinian monastery and later ordained as Bishop of Bobbia, then sent to Vercelli. His reputation as diplomat and peacemaker meant that he was often called on to settle disputes.

In 1205 he was appointed Patriarch of Jerusalem, but as the city was under the rule of the Saracens, he lived in Acre. Here he came into view of nearby Mount Carmel and the brothers there eventually approached him to write a rule for them, as he had for several other religious communities.

The saintly bishop complied and so the title of "lawgiver of Carmel" has been given to him.

> Each one shall remain in his cell or near it, meditating day and night on the Law of the Lord and watching in prayer, unless otherwise occupied. (St. Albert of Jerusalem)

He set out for them the observance of the canonical hours, their times of penance and of fasting, their vows of poverty, chastity and obedience, their need to work, to keep silence and for each to be the "slave of all".

In 1214, on the feast of the Exaltation of the Holy Cross, Bishop Albert was processing through the streets when he was accosted by the former Master of the Hospital of the Holy Spirit. Angered over his dismissal for immorality, the man stabbed Albert to death. His memory and the Rule lived on. It was approved by Pope Honorius III and later taken by the Brothers as they traveled to Europe in 1230.

Those of us who are Secular Carmelites living in "the world" all these centuries later remember him and give thanks to the Italian Bishop, transplanted to the Holy Land, who formed the structure and shape of the life we endeavor to lead.

May God be praised! And may St. Albert be at my side as I try to find, and lovingly embrace, the silence.

> But each person ought to create and build for himself an interior cloister, "a wall and a bulwark", a private desert, so as to meet God there in solitude and silence. (St. Albert of Jerusalem)

September 30, 2015

The last days of September have come and gone as I worked quickly in the garden—harvesting, preserving and then tidying up the spent plants. Then there was a pause for a grandson's birthday followed by a celebration for the feast of the Archangels. I have also been following along as Pope Francis visits America. The mind and spirit try to keep silent and prayerful, despite the busy days.

In the Carmelite calendar, today is a day of fast as we prepare ourselves to celebrate tomorrow's feast of St. Thérèse of the Child Jesus and the Holy Face. We have been looking forward to her feast with anticipation this past week as we pray a daily novena to our little saint. Then, when all is near readiness for breaking out into joy, we step back and prepare the body as well, for we are people of both soul and body and the penances we willingly perform have an impact on our life of the spirit.

> The ultimate goal of fasting is to help each one of us to make a complete gift of self to God. (Pope Benedict XVI)

I feel the fast today more than usual as I let yesterday's news penetrate further into my mind.

My mother stumbled descending a staircase and fell, breaking her hip. She lay inside on the bottom landing for three hours, trying with my father's help to get up before they finally gave in and called for assistance. When the ambulance arrived, she was whisked off to the hospital. Poor, dear mother. She sounded her old self on the phone, though, when she called to pass on the news to me. Why let a broken hip get you down?

So, today, I pack a suitcase, water the houseplants and figure out who will be feeding the chickens in my absence. I bow to the change in plans as I get a dozen eggs and a basket of vegetables and herbs ready to take along. If I plan things well, perhaps I might even have time to bake some bread, too, one loaf to leave for Andy and one to bring with me.

As I go through my busy day, I hear my Carmelite sisters and brothers speaking to me with encouragement, trying to help me see this day, this little "recalculating" in its proper light.

From Thérèse, herself:

Perfection consists in doing His will, in being what He wills us to be.

Lord, help me to do Your will. Mold me! And from St. Teresa Benedicta of the Cross:

I have an even deeper and firmer belief that nothing is merely an accident when seen in the light of God.

Lord, what good will You draw from this accident? Help me to see! And from our Holy Father, St. John of the Cross:

> After I have known it
> LOVE works so in me
> that whether things go well or badly
> love turns them to one sweetness
> transforming the soul in itself.
> (*Without Support Yet with Support*, stanza 3)

Lord, help me to find the sweetness, to find You!

October

October 1, 2015

Oh, how I look forward to this day every year! From the time I was a little girl, all those years ago in Missouri, I have loved St. Thérèse. My first introduction to her came in the form of some little *Treasure Box* books that I found in the back of church. They were sweetly illustrated and showed her as a young girl trying to please God, the One she loved. Each issue presented her at a different age and with her family all about. Later, as a young mother, I read *The Story of a Soul*, her autobiography, and came to know the little Carmelite on a deeper level. Some years passed and another book found its way to me: *I Believe in Love* by Fr. Jean d'Elbée.

What a profound impact this book had on me and my spiritual life. I have read and re-read it countless times, underlined and written notes in the margins. I have lent it to others and "prescribed" it for those I thought would benefit from the drawing out of the "Little Way" and from the insights into confidence, love and suffering.

For us, as Carmelites, today is a Feast and I had planned to celebrate accordingly with Mass and breakfast afterward with Lee. As part of my "recalculating", though, I will pack up the car and drive north after Mass to be with Mom as she recovers from her hip surgery.

Thankfully, though, Mont Deux Coeurs is on the way and I am blessed with the beauty, calm and silence of the monastery Mass.

Even the priest's homily helps place me in God's will this day as he expounds on the life and writings of St. Thérèse.

After Mass, I walk back to my car and drive to Vermont taking the scenic route in the valleys between the Berkshires and Green Mountains in the east and the Adirondacks in the west. I pass stone walls with pumpkins atop them, trees beginning to turn color and a succession of quaint, little towns.

It gives me plenty of time to think about Marie-Francoise Thérèse Martin, whom we know today as St. Thérèse of the Child Jesus and the Holy Face.

Though she must surely be among the most well-known of our modern saints, it takes some time and introspection to delve deeply into the life of this young "Doctor of the Church". She is not just a saint for pious children or a pleasant, saccharine, ornament of a doll. Thérèse grew up in a family, had her trials and difficulties, lost her mother at a young age and suffered from anxiety. Her father and her older sisters did not coddle her, though; they presented the spiritual life to her in its beauty and reality and in the discipline of life that it required. It is no wonder that God picked the sturdy "little flower" to bring her to a maturity of thought and love in her short twenty-four years so that, even today, so many experience the fragrance that her life and teachings emanate.

Thérèse, at 15, fought hard for her early entry into Carmel, lived her enclosed years there heroically and died a painful death from tuberculosis. But she also listened as God spoke to her in the silence of the cloister. In this silence she came to appreciate her littleness, to depend wholly upon God's love and mercy for everything, to have a supreme confidence in this love. She also came to recognize her mission and the immense good she would accomplish after her death, a good that would benefit the whole Church. Not only would she strew her roses upon priests and those gone astray, but especially upon the crowds who would read her writings and follow after her: the army of little souls.

So many books have been written about our Thérèse, so many have been attracted to her straight and simple path to intimacy with God, so many have been inspired to live obscure lives with a hidden importance as integral and essential foot soldiers in the army of Love. How delightful it will be one day to recognize each other as our "Little General" presents us to the emperor, our King of Kings.

Finally, I pull into the hospital parking lot and pray a chaplet of thanksgiving in the small chapel. Then after seeing mom as she comes out of surgery, another Evening Prayer of thanksgiving in the Surgical Waiting Room.

Mom, too, I know, is part of the little army, where even groggy from anesthesia she consoles her roommate Mary and prays a rosary with her.

Listen to what little Thérèse has to say in the fable about the weak little bird who, not having wings strong enough to soar in the heights, at least has eyes and a heart to gaze at the Son of love: "With bold abandonment, he remains gazing at his Divine Sun. Nothing can frighten him, neither wind nor rain; and if dark clouds come to hide the Star of love, the weak little bird will not move away, for he knows that on the other side of the clouds his Sun continues to shine."

"I am not always faithful, but I never get discouraged. I abandon myself into the arms of Jesus, and there I find again all that I have lost and much more besides."

"Since He has granted it to me to understand the love of the Heart of Jesus, I confess that He has chased all fear out of my heart. The memory of my faults humiliates me, leads me never to rely on my own strength, which is nothing but weakness; but even more this memory speaks to me of mercy and love. When we throw our faults, with a completely filial confidence, into the devouring furnace of love, how could they not be totally consumed?"

Diary of a Country Carmelite

Here we reach an essential point in the "little way." It is that a soul that is disposed to please Jesus in everything, that has committed everything to Him in freely committing its will—and these souls are more numerous than you might think—a soul that has made an oblation as a victim to merciful love … an act which the weakest souls are called to make because they are "more fitted to the operations of consuming and transforming love," such a soul, in its thirst for purity, can remember that it is continually purified in the fire of love. (Fr. Jean C.J. d'Elbée, *I Believe in Love*)

October 8, 2015

Mom is home from the hospital now, and I am cleaning and dusting and looking for some handles for the shower and other ways for my mother to be safely mobile. Thankfully, I am able to get to Mass in Whitehall in the morning. What a joy to be there on this, my 60th birthday, thanking God for everything.

In recent years, I have treasured the position of this day, snuck in the middle between the feast of St. Thérèse, a week ago, and St. Teresa, next week. I pray God for a little of each of their spirits of love and sacrifice. I know I will need them today.

And I do. Today it's Dad's turn for some scheduled surgery on his throat, so I leave Mom in the care of my sister-in-law, Gail, and go with Dad to the hospital.

In whatever God has called me to do today, whether it be as chauffeur, cook or housemaid, I can be fulfilling His will and joined to Him, whom I love. And I can bring Him in love to all those I meet today.

For a little over twenty years I have kept an unusual birthday tradition. I ask God for a particular virtue that I will concentrate on for the year ahead. His gift to me. For several weeks beforehand, I delve into my soul to see what I shall request or better, to find out what I particularly lack. This year, inspired by an antiphon from the Evening Prayer of St. Teresa's solemnity, I beg for a "*vast heart*".

> The Lord gave her wisdom and understanding beyond measure, and, a heart as vast as the sand on the seashore.

I do realize it is no simple gift, but I think, somehow, I will need that extreme largeness of heart this year. I will need the big-hearted love to keep me both unselfishly focused on the task at hand and absorbed in prayer. United to His Sacred Heart, I can find my place each day and bring His love to those I am privileged to serve.

> But You teach me that if the soul never separates itself from You, it can always remain absorbed in contemplation, even though apparently it is carrying out Martha's functions. In this way, O Lord, I intend and wish to exercise my apostolate: I shall radiate You, I shall give You to souls provided I do not separate myself from You, O Divine Source. (Elizabeth of the Trinity)

What a perfect way to spend my birthday. Thank you, Lord, for another year in which to serve You!

October, 15, 2015

I am still in the "Big Woods" of Hampton, New York, in the log house my father built those many years ago. After settling mom in with her breakfast, I head to morning Mass at Our Lady of Hope in Whitehall, thrilled that I have a chance to visit this beautiful old church once again. The celebrant on this feast of St. Teresa of Avila, a solemnity for us Carmelites, is a newly ordained priest from the Missionaries of the Most Holy Eucharist. Perfectly arranged, all the circumstances of my day are planned in advance by Divine Providence. Though I am missing a Day of Recollection with our Carmelites back home, I have this quiet morning with Our Lord and his holy priest. Deo gratias!

As our Carmelite saints are celebrated in the Liturgical calendar, it gives us a chance to beg their prayers, to study and ponder their lives and to marvel all over again, especially in the case of our "Holy Mother", on the amazing good they accomplished in their lives.

Teresa Sanchez Cepeda Davila y Ahumada was born in Avila in 1515, the third child of her father Don Alonso and his second wife, Dona Beatriz. They were pious parents and faithful Catholics and this little girl, with her natural intelligence and striking beauty, absorbed the atmosphere and ideals her parents lived. By all accounts she was a wild child, loved to ride horses and could unleash quite the temper when provoked. On the other hand, she was so struck with stories of the martyrs that when she was 6 or 7 she talked her older brother Rodrigo into accompanying her to the land of the Moors to seek martyrdom. When discovered on the road by an uncle, the missing children were returned home where the determined Teresa started building a hermit's hut instead.

She had a keen intelligence, loved to read and was one of those rare persons who seemed to entrance others with her personality. After reading the letters of St. Jerome, she was determined to enter the religious life. Her mother had died when she was thirteen, leaving behind a newborn, Juana. Her father, who was such an important part of this young girl's life, was loathe to part from her. So Teresa took matters into her own hands when she was twenty and left for the Carmelite convent of the Incarnation in Avila, a wrench she felt so enormously herself.

Thanks to the voluminous writings Teresa left behind and the foresight of the Carmelites who saved them all, we have a first-hand picture of her life, her mysticism, her concerns and her travels. Before all of this came years of ordinary convent life, marked by a serious illness shortly after she had taken her final vows. After a recovery, she would ever remain in frail health and endured sufferings of all sorts over the course of her life: heart troubles, severe nausea, tinnitus and tuberculosis, all in the 16th century when medical care and treatment left much to be desired.

Her prayer life suffered during these years, as well. The death of her father seemed to shake more resolve into her efforts, and Teresa once again made great strides up the "Way of Perfection". She was also aided by a number of holy Dominican and Jesuit spiritual directors who recognized her sanctity and facility in prayer and encouraged her in her progress toward Divine Union.

Teresa of Jesus came to realize that life in the Incarnation was not all it could be. Her ideas for reform began to take shape and then began another great period of activity, travels and writing, all marked by the suffering of misunderstandings, outright opposition, poverty and difficult roads.

Perhaps it is hard for us in our day of swift and easy travel to imagine just this one aspect of Teresa's indomitable drive and endurance. After 32 years as a cloistered nun, she set out on mule or in covered wagon over the next twenty years, suffering bumps, torturous climbs, inclement weather and the danger of highwaymen to found convent after convent of her "Discalced Carmelites"; setting up each in a spirit of austerity, deep prayer and love for Christ and His Church.

She called herself a poor writer and did not like to stop her activity and prayer, but under obedience she lost track of time as she wrote and wrote, sometimes with humor, often with digression, but always with a dedicated energy and obvious inspiration. Besides her *Life*, we have the book of her advice on prayer, *The Way of Perfection*; *The Book of Foundations*, the account of her travels as she sets up one convent after another; and her master work, *The Interior Castle*, describing the soul's journey from one *mansion* to another until the center, Union with God, is reached. There are other minor works as well, meditations and poetry and a huge body of letters. All give us a close-up view of St. Teresa of Jesus.

> By all accounts St. Teresa, the foundress from Avila, was a woman extraordinarily gifted, both naturally and supernaturally. In her were combined physical beauty, especially in her youth, and a charm of personality that neither age nor illness diminished. All witnesses seemed to agree that she was the type of woman no one can adequately describe in a few pages. She was one of those rare personalities who combine qualities that seem to exclude one another and are seldom found together in one individual. She loved tenderly and affectionately, yet would brook no nonsense from anyone. She possessed both a strong self- image and an astonishing humility. A born leader, she was yet completely obedient to her superiors. She could be a windmill of activity at one time and at another be lost in mystical contemplation. Though she was highly intelligent and amazingly efficient, she gravitated toward simple, humble men and women. (Thomas Dubay, S.M. *Fire Within*)

The first reformed convent, St. Joseph's in Avila, was begun in 1562; in 1568 the first house of the Friars' reform. Teresa remained active right up until her death in 1582. Her body remains incorrupt even today, with her heart showing marks of her "transverberation", the thrust of the angel's spear. I have even reverenced her glass-encased foot in a Carmelite church in Rome! She was canonized in 1622 and declared a Doctor of the Church in 1970.

After a busy day of doctor's appointments, cooking and laundry, I settle down in the evening and pick up some reading after Evening Prayer. Of course, there before me is a beautiful essay in the October issue of *Magnificat* by Anthony Esolen, which crowns the day and brings our Holy Mother into a sharper and sweeter focus.

> But isn't it remarkable? A thousand years from now, if the world is still here and man still lives upon it, ordinary and extraordinary people will be turning to Saint Teresa of Avila for her practical wisdom into things that soar infinitely beyond the practical. People who believe only in usefulness will be forgotten, useless as they are. The madness of our day will be forgotten, as a feverish dream. So I do hope.
>
> The Church has brought forth the most admirable women the world has known, and someday women themselves will become aware of it, and return to their beauty and their high calling. Out of the mouths of sisters in the cloister, and married women attending to the sweet duties of a human life, will come, has come, the praise of God. (Anthony Esolen, "How the Church Has Changed the World," *Magnificat*, October 2015)

I praise Him as I drift off to sleep, that I *am* aware of this great beauty and my *high calling*. And I thank St. Teresa that I am counted as one of her daughters.

October 18, 2015

The past few days have been busy ones. Nurses and lawyers coming to the house, trips to bring Dad to the doctor, then packing up and settling the house for a time when all of us will be away. Yesterday we put everything in order, packed up our suitcases and made the trip several hours south to Blandford; Mom and I in the first car and Dad in the second. We had some anxiety on the last leg home when we realized Dad wasn't behind us. We found out later that he had hit a curb and blown a tire, reminding us all of the time he was lost in Rome for several hours. Just when we were ready to get back in the car and retrace our steps, he pulled into the driveway. Ah, the joys and sorrows of family life!

This Sunday morning we are all together again as it snows softly on our drive home from Mass. Across the ocean, another family is being honored in Rome. It's the canonization day of Saints Louis and Zélie Martin, the parents of St. Thérèse of Lisieux. For the first time in Church history, a married couple will be raised to sainthood together; particularly fitting in our time of marked assault on family life and the dignity of the human person.

Why this particular husband and wife, and why now?

The Superior General of the Carmelite Order, Fr. Saverio Cannistra, wrote a letter to us all to answer those two questions and to give us added cause for joy.

Fr. Saverio says:

> This canonization is a further sign that the Lord gives us to confirm our faith and revitalize our journey as Carmelites.... We are living in an historical period marked by profound transformation, touching all areas of human life—morality, culture, religion, society, finance—at a global level, unleashing tension and fear.... The biblical vision of humanity, with its double division into male and female, and the understanding of its meaning with regard to life, are no longer a shared patrimony but are even questioned. At the centre of this battle for life there is the natural family, founded on the simple awareness of the providential difference between man and woman which, within a committed relationship based on committed love, allows human life to come into existence, be cared for and makes human life grow, not just for oneself, but for every human being. The canonization of the Martin husband and wife is a

sign of the times that ought to question us deeply since it has an epoch-making value.

That answers the second question, "why now?" But who were these two people and why have *they* been singled out from among millions of other married couples?

Zélie Guerin and Louis Martin were married in 1858; she was 27 and had a lace-making business, he was 35 and a watchmaker. Both had tried out religious life and found that, for one reason or another, God was not calling them to that vocation. Over the course of their married life they had nine children, suffered the grievous loss of four of them, and set themselves to raising the other five girls with love and devotion. Zélie died a painful death from cancer when she was 46 years old, whereupon Louis relocated the family from Alencon to Lisieux, so he had the help of their extended family in raising the girls. This very devout father concentrated all his strength on this task, and we can see, looking at the results, that he accomplished it admirably. Four daughters entered the Carmelite convent in Lisieux, including the youngest, Thérèse, while the fifth, Leonie, entered the Visitation monastery in Caen.

Even while suffering a humiliating illness which affected his mind, Louis held onto his love of God, repeating, "Everything for the greater glory of God" whenever he became aware of his surroundings. He lived seventeen years without his beloved Zélie, dying in August of 1877.

According to Fr. Saverio, there are "two traits that make them relevant" to married people of today. The first is to live out the "encounter" with each other, and the second is "marriage as a vocation".

> It is only by receiving oneself as a gift coming from God and learning to look at the other as an expression of the Father's love, that it is possible to build your own house on a firm foundation.

He sees the second trait as flowing from the first: to see each other as friends and allies in the living out of this conjugal life with all that it entails. With sanctity recognized as the goal, the serious husband and wife join hands and souls as partners on the journey, welcoming with joy any children God sends and rearing them with His help.

> Their canonization shows to all families, first of all to Christian families, the extraordinary beauty of ordinary things, when one's own story is received from God's hand and offered back to Him, with the reassuring knowledge that [as Zélie says in a letter] "the wisest and most simple thing in all this is to resign yourself to God's will and to prepare yourself beforehand to carry your own cross as bravely as possible." (Fr. Saverio Cannistra, OCD)

What perfect advice for me as I ponder these words, my hands in a soapy sink of dirty dishes. Strengthened for the task at hand by sharing the Eucharistic meal together, we settle in to see just what God has planned for us next, confident that with His grace we will be able to embrace it with a smile.

October 22, 2015

Mom and Dad have settled in nicely here; we are on a schedule to have a physical therapist come to the house to help Mom, and the lovely late October weather means Dad can hit a few golf balls around in the back yard. After breakfast this morning, I pull out the slow cooker, plop in a pork roast, some chopped garlic and onion and head out for Westfield. Today is the feast of Pope St. John Paul II, canonized just a year ago, and it is a joy to be able to go to Mass before my day at the library.

There is a strong connection between the Polish Pope and the Carmelites. In fact, if he had followed his original inclination, Karol Wojtyla would have become a Carmelite friar. The first time he tried to enter, he was told that due to the war, novices were not being accepted in Czerna, Poland. And the second time, when Karol was studying at the major seminary in Cracow and expressed a desire to Cardinal Sapieha to enter the Carmelites, he was advised to continue on the path he had begun. And so he did.

By his own admission, he told a group of Polish Carmelites in 1986, "*I was so close to being one of you.*"

But the Carmelite charism and the Carmelite saints were deeply rooted in his background and his psyche. Karol had a habit of going to confession at the Carmelite Church, wore the brown scapular from the time of his First Communion and chose St. John of the Cross to be the topic of his doctoral dissertation. He also had a lively devotion to Our Lady of Mount Carmel. "*She assisted me in finding the grace of my vocation.*" And of course, we all know he credited Our Lady with deflecting the bullet that was meant to end his life. What many may not know is that before the surgery to remove the bullet, Pope John Paul II insisted that the doctors leave his scapular around his neck.

As Pope he beatified 17 Carmelites, canonized five and declared one, St. Thérèse of Lisieux, a Doctor of the Church and another, St. Teresa Benedicta of the Cross, the Co-Patroness of Europe.

As if all this was not enough to prove our point, we must look at the example he gave in his life and pontificate to the practice of deep, contemplative prayer. Prayer preceded and ended each of his busy days and when he had "gone missing" in searches by the staff of the Pontifical household, he most likely would be found in the chapel, not at first being noticed, because he had prostrated himself before the altar. No doubt the many fruits of his pontificate can be found in the prayer that gave him the strength and inspiration to accomplish it all.

As I think of my parents and try to be of help to them these days, I ponder the great example of John Paul's last "encyclical", the witness our aging Pontiff, suffering mightily from Parkinson's disease, gave to the watching world. The witness of his life, poured out for all of us. Speaking of Mount Carmel in an Angelus address in 2000, he said:

> We are called to climb this spiritual mountain courageously and without pausing. Walking together with the Virgin, model of total fidelity to the Lord, we will not fear obstacles or difficulties. Sustained by her maternal intercession, like Elijah, we will be able to fulfill our vocation to be authentic "prophets" of the Gospel in our time. (Pope St. John Paul II)

November

November 2, 2015

It's four thirty in the afternoon and we've switched our clocks back again, so it shouldn't be surprising that the sun has already set. All is calm outside as I survey the landscape. There are a few patches of fading color among the trees, while in the foreground the chickens are pecking at what is left for them to eat in the barnyard. November is here already and, as we close the garden this time of year, so we also get ready to end the liturgical year.

But first, our two great November days to put us in our rightful place in the grand scheme of things. Yesterday, All Saints Day, fell on a Sunday, so we had a large contingent present to celebrate the Church Triumphant; all of us remembering our family members who led virtuous lives, our favorite canonized saints and all those unheralded folks from every time and place, known only to God, who sit "shoulder to shoulder" with their more famous neighbors—all enjoying the bliss of the presence of the Father, Son and Holy Spirit.

In the Office of Readings, St. Bernard speaks of his holy longing, "*But, I tell you, when I think of them, I feel myself inflamed by a tremendous yearning.*" He warns us, though, that, "*The Church of all the first followers of Christ awaits us, but we do nothing about it. The saints want us to be with them, and we are indifferent. The souls of the just await us, and we ignore them.*"

Looking at them and their proximity to Christ should fan into flame our meager desires and heat up our cold hearts. The saints themselves are so eager to help us, "*Thus what is beyond our own powers to obtain will be granted through their intercession,*" St. Bernard reminds us.

That's what a family does—we pray for one another.

As we did today on All Souls Day. Our compassion bids us to look kindly on the Church Suffering; on those who have died but have not yet had kindled in them the white-hot fires of perfect love. May our prayers today help to release a great throng from the purgatorian ante-chambers and escort them into the august halls of heaven.

In the background of my thoughts and prayers today I see a tiny baby and a young man in his prime. The little one, Nathan, born yesterday months before he should have been, is joining us in the Church Militant and we pray that he will have a strong hold on life and live to give joy to his parents and grandparents.

At the other end of the spectrum, we learned of the death of a young man, Christopher, who leaves behind a bereft wife and devastated parents.

I am related to neither the baby nor the young man, but I take their cases upon me as if they were close family. And so, in another way, they are. All members of one Body, one family in Christ.

Merciful Father, hear our prayers and console us. As we renew our faith in your Son, whom you raised from the dead, strengthen our hope that all our departed brothers and sisters will share in his resurrection, who lives and reigns with you and the Holy spirit, one God, for ever and ever. Amen. (Prayer, All Souls' Day)

November 5, 2015

For a while now, my Thursdays have followed the same pattern: morning Mass at St. Mary's in Westfield, then the drive back up the mountain to be at the library by the time we open at ten. This morning, though, I make a slight detour and head to the cemetery in Huntington. Continuing my prayer for the holy souls, I take advantage of the Church's offering of a plenary indulgence for the souls in Purgatory on the first eight days in November. It is a short visit; I park near Tim's grave, place myself in the Presence of God and try not to hurry through my prayer, remembering Tim, all our dear ones, the souls of those buried in this cemetery and all the souls suffering as they await the time of their purification to be completed. As always, I pray for those "orphan souls" who have no one to pray for them, then as the indulgence instructs, finish up with prayers for the pope.

It is always sobering to think, once again, on the end that we will all face. To try to use these days well that we have been given, so when we are called home by God we will have a short time in the waiting room, or even be ushered by our guardian angels directly into His presence. We can only hope!

Perhaps today's Carmelite was made aware of the importance of a life well-lived while quite young. That would explain so many things as we look at her life.

Frances d'Amboise was born in France in 1427. At the tender age of four she was betrothed to Pierre, the Duke of Brittany. As was often the custom, she went to live with her future mother-in-law, Jean of France, at this point. Frances was married at fifteen and endured another fifteen years of a difficult marriage. Pierre was not an easy person to live with. There was family feuding, and more seriously, Frances was treated poorly and at times even beaten by her husband. She did not abandon her faith or turn into a sour duchess but was remembered for her generosity to the poor, her devout faith and her love of adoration. She used her wealth to endow convents of Dominicans and Franciscans at Nantes and after the death of the Duke, desired to enter the Poor Clare Franciscans. At this point she met the Carmelite, John Soreth, who was making the rounds of the Carmelite monasteries in Brittany and beginning foundations of nuns. So, Frances deemed it was her vocation to help John found a monastery in France.

There was one rather large impediment, though. Pierre's father, the Duke of Brittany, wanted her to remarry and there was no shortage of suitors lined up to seek the hand of this beautiful young woman, including the future King Louis of France. After a three-year impasse, she boldly stood up during Mass and proclaimed a vow of perpetual chastity, causing the duke to finally acquiesce.

Frances helped John Soreth to found the community at Bondon near Vannes, bringing nine nuns from Liege to begin the new house. She herself entered a few years later, startling the Carmelites when she insisted on ignoring her noble birth and beginning as infirmarian. Eventually, Frances was elected prioress in 1473 and so many novices were attracted to the community that they moved to larger quarters in Nantes. In 1484 she resigned as prioress, wanting to spend her last days in simplicity and prayer. She died in 1485.

With John Soreth, Frances helped to work on legislation for the nuns, including the practice of frequent Communion and immersing oneself in loving prayer at all times. She was also an inspired spiritual director and left her nuns some wise words to guide their lives.

Whatever the troubles and difficulties that weigh you down, bear them all patiently and keep in mind that these are the things which constitute your cross. Offer your help to the Lord and carry the cross with Him in gladness of heart. There is always something to be endured, and if you refuse one cross, be sure that you will meet with another. (Blessed Frances d'Amboise)

No matter our own particular sufferings, we can each take this advice to heart and repeat these words after Frances:

Lay everything down at the foot of His cross, and rest there in peace.

Amen.

November 6, 2015

As I dress for a funeral this morning, I also don my "armor" of emotional detachment, prepared to get through the day for my friend, Pat, despite the memories these funerals always bring to the surface. Pat's son, Christopher, will be prayed over and sent off to his final resting place with all military solemnity, as befits one who has served with honor and valor in his military career. What a blessing to have this Mass said to beg God's mercy for him and His compassion for the family that is left behind. I add my prayers to the church full of others and have ample time to ponder and pray more on the drive back home.

I stop in Westfield where I meet up with Mom so we can both get our hair cut; an ordinary activity following such a sober event. I have more time though, sitting patiently in the chair as I hear the snip, snip of the scissors, to place myself in the Presence of God, offering up this, too, for Pat and her husband, Paul. My imagination transports me to Spain while thinking of today's Carmelite, who lived over a hundred years ago and across an ocean, but who nonetheless was so attuned to those in her birthplace and to all of their ordinary needs and trials.

Josefa Naval Girbes was born into a loving, Catholic family in the small agricultural town of Algemesi, known for citrus production, in the province of Valencia in Eastern Spain. She was born in 1820 and baptized on the day of her birth, December 11. Four siblings followed in her wake and, as the eldest daughter, she became adept in the care of the house and the family. She did not attend school but was taught to read and write at home and became expert in the art of embroidery. Josefa was a particularly devout child, receiving her First Communion when she was nine, two years earlier than was customary at that time. There was only one Catholic church in Algemesi, a Dominican monastery, and life revolved around home and the parish.

She needed all her spiritual maturity and her household skills when, at thirteen, she took over the care of the family after her mother's death. At prayer in front of the altar, she was assured by the Blessed Virgin that she would always have *her* spiritual motherhood to guide and protect her.

The family moved into the home of her maternal grandmother where Josefa helped raise the little ones and became an ideal house-keeper. She was inspired to make a vow of perpetual chastity when she was eighteen and entered the Discalced Carmelite Third Order, today called the Secular Carmelites.

When her grandmother became bedridden, Josefa added the care of the sick one to her other duties. She was twenty-seven when her grandmother died; now the household included her father, her Uncle Joaquin and a younger brother and sister. Later, her widowed brother Vincente came back home to live with them. But, really, all of Algemesi was her family.

Josefa sought out the sick, noticed who needed food and who required the counsel to baptize their infant. She consulted with her trusted spiritual director and received his permission to open a free embroidery school in her home. Young women came to work on their trousseau and perfect their skills with the needle. More importantly, she taught them with reading and prayer, the Catholic life of a virtuous woman and helped many discern their vocation, either to marriage or the religious life. It even came under the notice of the local bishop that this little town of 8,000 had an unusually high percentage of women who had chosen to enter the convents of the region.

> Josefa Navel Girbes is an exceptional mistress of secular holiness: a model of Christian life in her heroic simplicity; a model of parish life. Her entire life proves how one can reach holiness in all states of life in a total consecration to God and in a selfless love for one's brothers and sisters, even while living in the world. Without extraordinary gifts an exceptional woman in her genuine simplicity as a daughter of the people. She carried out her duties faithfully, in intense union with God, in the midst of the ordinary circumstances of her working day. (General Promoter of the Faith, Monsignor Petti, at the conclusion of the Theological Consultors' Examination)

> Josefa told her "students": "*Reach holiness no matter what the cost.*" And then showed them how to accomplish this: "*The fulfillment of our duties is the way; the degree of love with which we comply is the measure of the virtue our soul has.*"

She arose early each morning to attend the first Mass of the day, then spent time in mental prayer in the quiet monastery before heading home to tidy the house and prepare for her students. The young women sewed and prayed with her, but also were taught with long periods of silence. In her walks around the town she saw who needed clean clothes, who had a torn shirt in need of mending, who was deathly ill and needed the Sacrament of the Sick. Her generosity was sacrificial, and more than once she brought home to live with her children whose parents had died. She tended the sick during a cholera epidemic in 1885. Her reputation in the town brought those in need of counsel, as well, to her doorstep, and all went away ready to bear a cross or make an important decision.

On Sunday afternoons, the work was put away, but the young women still gathered after the evening Mass when they were instructed in the love of God. In the spring or summer, they walked to an orchard Josefa had been given, "The Orchard of La Torreta" where among the citrus trees they strolled and listened to her wise voice, *"My daughters, let us pretend that we are here like the Lord with his apostles. I in His name, tell you: 'Be good, do everything out of love; have much charity between you; live with abnegation and with a spirit of sacrifice.'"*

Josefa was beloved by the Dominican friars of her parish as she collaborated with them in the instruction of the people, but also appreciated for sewing and cleaning the liturgical vestments and embroidering those used for great solemnities. Ever humble, Josefa and her followers cleaned the church, too. Her example is remembered even today as descendants of these young women continue the practice.

She died, after a painful illness, when she was 74 on February 24, 1893, and at her request was buried in the Carmelite habit, which encloses her incorrupt body. Pope St. John Paul II beatified her in 1988.

A small photo of Blessed Josefa sits on a shelf in my sewing room and as I pass by it, I remember this little seamstress and beg her for the grace to keep busy with all the work my hands find to do, but most especially with the work of loving God and loving whomever is near at hand and needing my help, whether it is a grieving friend or my own mother or a stranger in the grocery store who needs a smile. May Josefa help us embroider a beautiful life!

November 7, 2015

It is another busy Saturday with a variety of things that need doing. I make my list in the morning: prepare for our trip to Alabama, vacuum the rugs, send a card to a sick friend, call Mom and Dad to make sure all is going well on their drive back home, pull some hamburger out of the freezer for the meatball soup. Another day.

Of course, it is a given that the day will begin with prayer and Mass. How else does one live this life with all its concerns and stress? When I read about the Carmelite on today's liturgical calendar, though, I think I have it pretty easy.

Francis Palau y Quer, like yesterday's Carmelite, was born in a small agricultural town in Spain, Aytona, in 1811. He was the seventh of nine children; his parents were farmers, but again, as devout Catholics, life had a higher meaning than their absorption in the work of each day. The rosary was prayed together in the evenings after all the farm chores, and on Sundays the father and all nine of his children sang in the parish choir during Mass. What beautiful little details that help us to get a glimpse into their ordinary lives, to see them as real people.

Francis was intelligent and a good student and at age seventeen entered the diocescan seminary in Lerida on a full scholarship. In the course of his studies, though, after meeting some Carmelite friars, he realized he was being called to enter into the religious life of the Order. And so it was that after four years he relinquished his scholarship in order to enter the Carmelites in Barcelona on November 14, 1832. He was given the name Francisco of Jesus, Mary and Joseph. Two years later, after more study and formation, he was ordained a deacon.

Meanwhile, Spain was experiencing the beginnings of a period of great persecution for the Catholics within its borders. In July of

1835, riots broke out and an angry mob attacked the monastery in Barcelona, burning it to the ground. Later, Francis would remember:

> When I made my religious profession, the revolution already had in hand the firebrand for burning all the religious establishments.... I was not ignorant of the pressing peril to which I exposed myself nor of the rules of foresight that would have saved me from it. Nevertheless, I dedicated myself by solemn vows to a state whose rules I believed I could practice until death, independently of all human events. (*The Solitary Life*)

With all the other friars and religious, Francis escaped harm, but the community was now disbanded and he fled back home to Aytona, where he was prepared from a distance for his ordination, which took place in April of 1836. What would happen now, though? He was 25, but with no community or superiors to direct him. He had prayer and he was able to offer the Holy Sacrifice of the Mass, so properly "armed" he practiced the life of an active contemplative, wandering in rural Catalonia and Aragon, living in caves and preaching to the people in his persecuted Spain, encouraging them in the practice of their faith during a time when it was being shouted from the housetops that it was of no value to believe in God or to serve Him.

Watching the political situation closely, Fr. Francis crossed the Pyrenees into France in 1840 when he deemed it was too dangerous to remain in Spain. He lived again the solitary life of a hermit, encouraged others and added writing to his activity, publishing a book called, "The Soul Struggling with God". Thinking it might be safe, he returned home to Aytona and resumed his preaching there, but this time was accused of "upsetting the public order". So, in 1846 he hiked back across the border into France, where the political and religious situation was not much better, as he was to discover.

It was now time for France to experience her own trials. In 1848 the French were still roiling from another period of revolution. Despite criticism from the local bishop and active persecution, Fr. Francis persevered in prayer and the solitary life, writing and begging God's mercy upon His suffering people.

> If Christ's prayer and the fruits of his redemptive work are to be applied to any nation or people, or if the gospel message is to enlighten them and they have someone to administer the Sacraments, it is indispensable that someone or even many persons should have previously won them over and reconciled them to God by earnest entreaties and supplications, by prayers and sacrifices. For this purpose, among others, the Eucharistic sacrifice is offered on our altars. This sacred Victim which we present to the Father every day, accompanied by our own petitions, is not simply destined to recall the memory of the life, passion, and resurrection of Jesus Christ but also to oblige God in his goodness to show his graciousness in applying the graces of his Son's redemption to the nation, province, city, village, or to whatever persons or person for whom the Mass is offered.

The year 1851 saw him back in Spain and still with no Carmelite community. He accepted an appointment from the Bishop of Barcelona to serve as spiritual director to the seminarians there and was assigned to the parish of St. Augustine where he started the "School of Virtue" to instruct the adults. When the government heard about it, they shut it down and Fr. Francis was arrested and transported to the island of Ibiza, off the coast of eastern Spain. We have already seen that he could practice his ministry anywhere and so it was on the island. For the six years he remained banished in Ibizia, he found solitude and prayer but also built a hermitage, established a vegetable garden and orchard, constructed a Marian sanctuary, undertook missions among the people, reorganized some hermits on a neighboring island, founded a Third Order of Discalced Carmelites among the lay people and wrote an autobiography! Any ground was fertile ground for this hard-working priest.

As he once said, "*I will go wherever the glory of God calls me.*"

His later years, back in mainland Spain, were also times of great productivity. In 1867, Fr. Francis was appointed director of all Carmelite third orders and wrote a Rule for them, founded two communities of Carmelite nuns, established a weekly paper, assisted the sick and worked as an exorcist. During an outbreak of typhus in 1872, he aided those who were ill, finally himself dying of pneumonia at the age of 60, never having shirked his duty or found the easy way out of any difficulty.

Fr. Francisco Palau was beatified by Pope St. John Paul II in 1988 and remains the beloved spiritual father of his Teresian Carmelite Missionaries, who serve on four continents, and the Carmelite Missionaries, active in 40 countries around the world.

Our son, Fr. Tom, is flying to a conference in Dubai today, where he must not wear a Roman collar or any other garb that would identify him as a priest. In my motherly concern for his safety, I think about Blessed Francisco's own mother. Did she follow his travels and travails with worry or did *she* bequeath *him* the undivided heart that he, seemingly, possessed?

May this holy mother and her heroic son inspire me to have no fear for my son and to move forward in whatever direction I need to go when God directs me.

November 8, 2015

The routine is the same most Sundays. Andy and I share a quiet breakfast together, then we drive down the hills to 10:30 Mass. It is good to see our family there and the Church friends that have become like family, too. We greet them after Mass and hear of their joys and sorrows. In the heart of family life is always born the seed of our own vocation.

As it was for Blessed Elizabeth of the Trinity, whose memorial falls on our Carmelite calendar today. She was born Elizabeth Catez in France in 1880, the first child of a decorated military man and his devout wife. Another sister, Marguerite, was born several years later. There were numerous moves with the Captain's military service, but Elizabeth's parents had forged a strong family bond that was further strengthened by their Catholic faith, so despite the ordinary trials of life, they flourished, even when death came unexpectedly. Captain Catez died when Elizabeth was seven and the family was about to move to Dijon, so sorrow came early to her.

As a young girl she also had some strong character traits to overcome, being known to exert her temper forcefully when she was crossed. As with many young saints, the time of her First Confession and then later, First Communion, proved to be a deepening of grace that showed in her ability to conquer these faults more readily. The family's life in Dijon settled into a period of calm with studies, travel and music lessons. Both Sabeth and Guite were excellent pianists and spent many long hours practicing and giving concerts.

The Catez family home was quite near the Carmel of Dijon, so Sabeth made frequent visits to the chapel there and knew the nuns well. Despite her mother's objections she was being called ever more deeply to the life of the cloister, the life of deep prayer. No doubt due to her close association with the Carmel, she was able to read an early version of Sr. Thérèse of the Child Jesus's *Story of a Soul.* Like Thérèse, who had died several years earlier, she felt a strong pull to interior prayer and the "one thing" necessary, union with God.

May nothing distract me from You, neither noise nor diversions. Oh my Master, I would so love to live with You in silence.

207

But what I love above all is to do Your will, and since You want me still to remain in the world, I submit with all my heart for love of You. I offer You the cell of my heart; may it be Your little Bethany. Come rest there. (St. Elizabeth of the Trinity)

Her mother finally acquiesced and Elizabeth entered the Dijon Carmel a few days after her twenty-first birthday. She blossomed in the peace and quiet of the cloister, at last able to devote her whole self to her God, the Trinity who was calling her, able to enter into the silence to find and encounter God.

It seems to me that I have found my heaven on earth, because my heaven is You, my God, and You are in my soul. You in me, and I in You—may this be my motto. (St. Elizabeth of the Trinity)

Sr. Elizabeth of the Trinity was to spend only five years in Carmel, and, like Thérèse, she spent the last of these days in great pain, but also great resignation, as she suffered from Addison's disease. Close to the end she still had the presence of mind to write a beautiful "retreat" for her sister, Guite. Thanks to this testament and the other letters, poems and songs she composed, we can still see today the beauty of this dear soul, called to be a "Laudem Gloriae", Praise of the glory of God.

Saint Elizabeth sees us as musical instruments capable of joining in the Holy Trinity's great hymn of praise. This music is beautiful, but to produce it, the Holy Spirit must "tune" us first. This is painful. As long as we get caught up in internal emotional storms or else allow ourselves to be distracted by things that are not God's will, we are out of tune. Conversely the more our interior life is in harmony with His mystery, the more beautiful the praise we are able to offer. (Dr. Anthony Lilles, STD, Novena to St. Elizabeth of the Trinity)

May God tune us all, each and every member of His dear family, so that together with St. Elizabeth, we may harmonize in that great eternal hymn of praise.

November 14, 2015

After a day of fasting yesterday to prepare soul and body, we put on the festive clothes today for a grand celebration: All Carmelite Saints. It feels like I have reached the peak of the mountain I have been climbing all year. Naturally—or more properly, supernaturally—Holy Mass comes first and to set the day apart in the best way, I travel a little farther to the Visitation Monastery where Lee will join me for Mass. The rest of our community is scattered over several counties and three states, but we will celebrate as a community of two, physically, and as a congregation of thousands if we consider all the Carmelite friars, nuns and seculars around the world. The numbers increase exponentially, however, in the grandest scheme when we count both those beatified and canonized, and those unnamed crowds of Carmelites enjoying the presence of their Creator in heaven.

Oh, happy day!

The silence and the distance once again prepare me for the sublime liturgy in the hills of Tyringham as we all enter in to our little heaven on earth.

I feel I have been drawing closer and closer to our Carmelite saints as the year has proceeded, in the way one does when getting to know a friend in a deeper way over time.

One of my brother Carmelites, now with God, and himself on the path to beatification once said:

The more I study the life and works of our saints, the more
I love them with greater attachment, like parents or older

brothers and sisters, and I appeal to them with complete assurance that my prayers will be answered. (Père Jacques of Jesus)

I see each dear soul more familiarly now and know for certain that they are encouraging me to keep climbing the ladder to Union, chiding me to detach myself from the ties to material things that hold me back. The saints are our cheering section along the road race, the crowd waving signs along the finish line; friends I haven't met yet in person, from every century and each country around the world, pulling for me and rooting for me to pick up the pace and not give in to fatigue or thirst.
Fr. Gabriel says it best:

> What is of the greatest importance is to know that union with God is not reserved for a small number of privileged souls; God calls every soul of good will to union with Himself, regardless of the way by which He chooses to lead it. Hence, the ordinary way, "the little way," as St. Thérèse of the Child Jesus called it, or the "carriage road," according to St. Maria Bertilla, leads just as surely to divine union. Instead of preoccupying ourselves about the way, let us rather concern ourselves with striving to be completely generous, for only souls who give themselves wholly to God reach union with Him. (Fr. Gabriel of St. Mary Magdalene, OCD, *Divine Intimacy*, 362)

Our Holy Mother, St. Teresa of Jesus, leads the great throng and reminds those of us here below how we can hope to join the procession:

> O my God, how precious is the union which the soul attains with You, after having established itself in submission to Your will. Oh, how much to be desired is this union, in which we resign our wills to the will of God! Happy the soul which has attained it, for it will live peacefully both in this life and in the next, for, apart from the peril of losing You, O Lord, or

of seeing You offended, there is nothing that could afflict it, neither sickness nor poverty nor even death, for this soul sees clearly that You know what You are doing better than it knows itself what it desires! (*The Way of Perfection*)

November 16, 2015

Just as the love of Christ and the service of the Blessed Virgin Mary have brought us together in a single family, fraternal charity unites those of us still striving to lead a life of allegiance to Jesus Christ in this world, and those already awaiting the vision of God in purgatory. Today the whole Order commends our departed brothers and sisters to God's mercy through the intercession of Our Lady, sure sign of hope and consolation, and begs for their admission to the courts of heaven. (Carmelite Supplement, Liturgy of the Hours)

Today, we celebrate the Commemoration of All Carmelite Souls, since yesterday the original date, was a Sunday. As in the first two days in November in the Universal Church, so we have these two days together in the middle of the month, to remember, to honor and to cover with prayer those gone before us.

This morning I drive to another monastery for Mass, the Dominicans, almost an hour to the east. Together with my fellow Carmelite, Maureen, we pray for all those in our own little community who have died, and for all the other Carmelites in our "family" throughout the world who are waiting for a table in the great banquet hall. Just as a family prays for a dear one who has died, we join our prayers to those of our other brothers and sisters, fathers and mothers, to beg God's mercy that the wait will not be long.

Diary of a Country Carmelite

After Mass we head across the street for breakfast and conversation. It is my turn to write about Maureen and her family for our community newsletter, so over our hot mugs of coffee and tea, I get to know her better as I scribble away on my notepad. What mercy God has shown in each person's life and what trials He has given us so that our offering to Him might have more weight and love behind it.

Today our prayer is raised up, in large part, for those we don't know and never had a chance to meet, whose stories I will never write. United in our Catholic faith and with the additional bonds of our Carmelite family, they are dear to us and we gladly undertake this work for their benefit. One day we will all be in the same position and will ourselves be so grateful for someone else's prayers.

> For love of our Lord I beg them to remember how quickly everything comes to an end, and what a favor the Lord has done in bringing us to this Order, and what a punishment anyone who starts any kind of relaxation will deserve. They must always look at the race we are descended from—that race of holy prophets. What a number of saints we have in heaven who have worn this habit of ours! We must have the holy audacity to aspire, with God's help, to be like them. The struggle will not last long, but the outcome will be eternal. (St. Teresa of Avila, *The Book of Her Foundations*)

November 18, 2015

I have a guest coming for lunch today, so I go over the menu in the morning: Minnesota Wild Rice Soup, Rye Bread and Baked Apples. There are some vegetables to chop and the bread dough must be mixed and set to rise. After a few hours the food is all prepared and

I put the finishing touches on the table and pull the tea pot down from the shelf.

Today is Tim's 26th birthday and my long-time friend, Priscilla, is driving up from Connecticut to spend the day with me. We will start with noon Mass together in Westfield and then drive back to Blandford for lunch. It is comforting to have another mother with me today who has suffered the loss of a son. Priscilla's John suffered from the time he was four from leukemia, spent time in various hospitals across the country and was on a plan of treatment that looked promising when it became apparent that the end was near. He was just eight years old. Being a sweet, innocent child, he was open to God's love and had that beautiful, child's faith.

Tim's story was a different one, but even at fifteen he held tightly onto his own innocence and faith. We two mothers bless God today for our sons, for that faith which guides us and gives us purpose and helps us to find the joy, even in sorrow.

Last December Priscilla gave a talk to a gathering of Catholic women and told John's story with a beauty and a spiritual depth that amazed us all. In the introduction she told us:

> Grief has its season, but in the Christian contract, Joy secures an override clause. Joy does not annihilate grief, but makes it bearable, until the day when He shall wipe away all tears.
>
> But even in the grief of losing a loved one, there is something curious. With most grief there is the tiniest seed of joy. Let me explain. Most every grief is accompanied by a deep longing. Our Faith nurtures that seed of yearning. And the yearning makes us mindful that we are not in a state of rest, we are in Pilgrim mode, moving towards something. If we are mature Christians, we know we are yearning for that place where all things are made whole. The yearning is more ardent when we yearn to be with a loved one, but the fact of

its existence gives us some joy in the contemplation of that communion....

So even in grief, we are Pilgrims on the road to Joy, because we are Pilgrims to the source of joy." (Priscilla McCaffrey, *When H is for Hematology ... It Is Also for Heartache, Holiness and Hope*)

We will be welcomed one day by John and Tim to that Joy. In the meantime, we keep yearning and trying to fill each day with as much love as we can muster. It is the only way.

May God's love guide us all our days and help us to see His will and all that He permits as signs of that gracious love. Happy Birthday, Tim!

November 19, 2015

I headed down the hill this morning in heavy fog and a light drizzle. After morning Mass, I retraced my path and found that the fog had lifted just a little. Today was one of my library days, so I turned into the little lane in the center of town and pulled into the library parking lot instead of continuing on home. Thursdays are usually a little quiet and so it was today. I catalogued some books, straightened up a few shelves and pulled out the children's Thanksgiving books to display.

The highlight of the day was a visit from a mom with her three young children. The two oldest, a girl and a boy with the sweet bloom of innocence upon their faces, made their way over to my desk and drew some pictures of their home as I peppered them with questions.

I thought about them later as I was reading about today's Carmelite saint. He lived on another continent and spoke another language, but he had a great interest in little ones like these two, even when his life had turned into a great trial, by all outward appearances.

Joseph Kalinowski was born in 1835 in what is now Vilnia, Lithuania, but was then, Vilna, a city in Russian Poland. Joseph was taught at home early on, then when he was nine, he went to the "College of the Nobility", where his father was a professor of mathematics. At seventeen he wanted to enter the religious life, but his father encouraged him to earn a college degree first, so he traveled to St. Petersburg, where he ended up studying at the college of Military Engineering. He was a student of great talent and upon completion of his degree, he was commissioned as a Lieutenant in the Russian Engineering Corps, eventually helping to design and build a railway line.

However, the political situation in the country changed drastically and in 1863 he resigned to join the Polish rebellion against Russia. Joseph was arrested, tried, and sentenced to death, but this decision was later commuted to ten years hard labor in Siberia.

Can you imagine a journey of nine months on foot to Siberia? Joseph spent nine years in the slate mines but didn't lose his peace or his faith. He encouraged his fellow prisoners by his words and example and helped prepare their children to receive their First Communion. Disregarding all movements toward anger and resentment, he exhibited a great serenity and, through his prayers and sacrifices for others, gave them hope.

When Joseph's sentence had been served, he was released but was forbidden from living in any major Polish city. Here we see again God's hand at work, guiding the destiny of one man who was devoted to Him and another who was seeking Him. In Paris, Joseph served as a tutor for three years to Prince Augustus Czartoryski, and in the course of those years, where he served as "father, mother, nurse, brother, companion and caretaker" to the young prince, who suffered from tuberculosis, he laid the groundwork for the young man's own priestly vocation. Prince Augustus eventually went on to join the Salesian order and was beatified by Pope St. John Paul II in 2004. The connection was favorable to Joseph as well, for he met a princess, a relative of the young prince, who introduced him to the writings of St. Teresa of Avila and St. John of the Cross. (The princess later went on to enter Carmel herself.)

Diary of a Country Carmelite

Joseph, following a circuitous route, was finally ready to realize his own vocation in 1877, when he entered the Carmelite Order in Graz, Austria and took the name Raphael of St. Joseph. He studied theology in Hungary before being ordained in 1882 in Czerna, the site of the only Carmelite house in Poland.

Fr. Raphael used the twenty-five years of his priestly life to great advantage, writing books on Carmelite spirituality, founding monasteries of nuns, and a monastery, college and seminary in Wadowice, Poland. He was also inspired to work with the schismatic Russian Orthodox along the Polish border with Russia. In all his areas of labor he was known as a man of deep prayer who practiced a heroic self-denial and encouraged the people in a love of the sacrament of Penance. Dying in 1907 of tuberculosis, Raphael was beatified by his fellow countryman and Wadowice native, Pope St. John Paul II in 1983 and canonized by him in 1991.

What a striking example for us to be always seeking God's will in whatever circumstances we find ourselves among the young or old who cross our path.

> I like to find at least a few moments each day spent in doing good for others out of love for God. These few moments, almost unnoticeably used, bring something like rays of peace and comfort behind them; they unite us with people and God by a pure feeling of tender sweetness. (St. Raphael Kalinowski)

November 26, 2015

Another Thanksgiving Day dawns bright and promising, but instead of the usual cold, drab, brown surroundings, we have the warmth and beauty of Alabama on the Gulf to cheer us. Andy and I start the day at the little church that has become "home" to us here, Our Lady of the Gulf, to celebrate Mass with a dear family that we do not know and yet do know on another, deeper level. We thank God together for the past year and for all the blessings He has provided, of the ordinary and not-so-ordinary sort.

Back with our family, we prepare food with a great camaraderie, a fair amount of joking and that sense of anticipation that always precedes a feast. It reminds us of the good times we had together when we were in Rome for Fr. Tom's ordination and cooked together in the apartment kitchen. All happily working in peace and then sitting down to a banquet, even if it was of the simplest sort.

I get the grandsons to help me with a little project. We roll balls of bread dough into long ropes and lay them next to one another to resemble a sheaf of wheat, then braid some pieces to wrap around the middle. It comes out of the oven later—a thing of beauty—and we place it in the center of the table as a visual representation of all we have to be thankful for: "our daily bread". We begin with prayer to our Heavenly Father for all the bounty He has given us, for the faces around the table, for the chance to travel here, for the beauty of this little spit of land jutting out into the Gulf of Mexico, for the love around the table.

After the sun sets and the stars become visible, I slip out of the house and walk towards the beach; the sound of the crashing waves guides me and the solitude becomes an aide to prayer. I pull a rosary out of my pocket and offer another sort of thanksgiving. For God, the Creator of all this beauty, for His grace that has preceded and followed all our comings and goings, for the ability to recognize Him in all things, for the knowledge and opportunity to give thanks back to Him in prayer, for my Carmelite vocation. For everything.

We must, then, disengage ourselves from everything so as to approach God interiorly and even in the midst of occupations withdraw within ourselves. Although it may be for only a moment that I remember I have that Company within myself, doing so is very beneficial. (St. Teresa of Avila, *Way of Perfection*, 29:5)

November 29, 2015

Yesterday was an epic travel day for us. Andy and I left Gulf Shores, Alabama and after stops in Nashville and Baltimore finally landed at Bradley Airport in Hartford, Connecticut, where our son Paul met us and drove us the last leg of the journey home. It was a trip of a little over 1,300 miles and a long and tiring day, but when I compare it to travel in the 17th century it was like a walk around the block.

Today's two Carmelites, Blessed Denis and Redemptus, could readily attest to that. They suffered martyrdom in Indonesia in 1638 after a lengthy and grueling sea voyage from Goa in western India.

Who were these two young men and how did they manage to be together on a ship with a diplomat trying to bring peace to an unstable part of the world?

Thomas Rodriguez de Cunha was born in Portugal in 1598 and went on to become a soldier, rising to captain and commander of the guard. In his travels he came to know the Carmelites in Goa, part of Portuguese India, and there he switched professions, becoming a lay brother known as Redemptus of the Cross. As porter, he opened doors instead of hacking them with a sword, and as sacristan, took care of the altar and sanctuary. Both very tame jobs compared to his life in the military. A likeable young fellow, he joked before his last voyage that perhaps his portrait should be painted since it was possible he could become a martyr. I wonder if anyone took him seriously and got out their brushes and paint.

Pierre Berthelot was two years younger, born in 1600 in a seaport town in France. Perhaps it is no wonder he was drawn to the sea. He achieved some fame as navigator and cartographer and this handsome man, known for his sharp mind and spirit of adventure, had already come far in his early 30s, having been knighted by the King of Portugal and named "Master Navigator and Cosmographer of the Orient". Like Br. Redemptus, though, he was being drawn to something deeper than the ocean; to Someone. When he was 34, he also entered the Carmelite Order in Goa where he had been a friend of the prior, Fr. Philip of the Trinity. Pierre, now known as Denis of the Nativity, began his studies towards the priesthood and settled in to a quieter way of life. For a little while, anyway.

In 1638 a diplomatic mission was being planned by the Portuguese, and the Carmelites were asked if Denis could accompany them as navigator. His ordination was advanced so he could serve the men as chaplain on their voyage. And his superiors gave Br. Redemptus to him as a companion. The distance which Andy and I traveled yesterday took these men a month, and instead of being met with gladness in Sumatra, they were imprisoned upon landing.

Each man saw this turn of events as an opportunity to offer their God a fitting sacrifice and witness as their captors tried to entice them to convert to Islam. Fr. Denis and Br. Redemptus remained steadfast during torture. Calmly they walked to the beach for their execution. Br. Redemptus was killed first, then all of the ship's crew except for the ambassador who was ransomed later. As he had wished, Fr. Denis was the last to die. This allowed him to encourage and pray for the men, before himself being beheaded with a scimitar.

These two martyrs became well known in the 17th and 18th centuries and served as the "seed bed" for the conversions that followed in Sumatra. They were missionaries of another sort, but nonetheless fruitful. They are also men that we can look to today for inspiration and help in our troubled global times.

Diary of a Country Carmelite

Father, we celebrate the memory of Blessed Denis and Redemptus who died for their faithful witnessing to Christ. Give us the strength to follow their example, loyal and faithful to the end. We ask this through our Lord, Jesus Christ, your Son, who lives and reigns with you and the Holy Spirit, one God, for ever and ever. Amen. (Prayer, feast day of Blessed Denis and Redemptus, Martyrs)

December

December 3, 2015

There is a crisp, sharp quality to the air this morning with a wild wind gusting intermittently, at one moment moving gently over the water puddles left from yesterday's rain, and at the next furiously howling and picking up the piles of stray leaves at the road's edge.

How often our interior life follows suit—moving from calm to agitation; blown about by the wind of our daily interactions with others and by our own busyness.

I have stopped by the river on my way home from Mass this morning, having the gift of thirty extra minutes before I must be at the library. I want to prolong my thanksgiving after Communion and it's sometimes more productive to pray in the quiet car than in the church with the comings and goings of the men and women, the footsteps and whispered conversations. I want to be truly quiet; to let the stillness be perceptive, to listen to the Guest of my soul free from any distractions.

In this morning's Gospel, Matthew puts these words on the lips of Jesus, *"Not everyone who says to me, "Lord, Lord" will enter the kingdom of Heaven, but only the one who does the will of my Father in Heaven."*

The theme began this morning in my half hour of mental prayer, encouraged by Fr. Gabriel of St. Mary Magdalene, OCD, who equated sanctity with the *perfect* accomplishment of God's will.

And to show that the souls who are most closely united to Him, the ones He loves most, are precisely those who do the will of God, He does not hesitate to say: "Whosoever shall do the will of My Father, that is in heaven, he is my brother, and sister, and mother" (Mt 12:50).

The saints learned in the school of Jesus. St. Teresa of Avila, after having received the most sublime mystical communications, did not hesitate to declare, "The highest perfection consists not in interior favors, or in great raptures, or in visions, or in the spirit of prophecy, but in the bringing of our wills into conformity with the will of God that, as soon as we realize He wills anything, we desire it ourselves with all our might, and take the bitter with the sweet" (*Foundations*, 5). St. Thérèse of the Child Jesus echoes this statement, "The more joyfully [souls] do His will, the greater is their perfection" (*Story of a Soul*, 1).

True love of God consists in adhering perfectly to His holy will, not desiring to do or to be other than what God indicates for each of us, to the point of becoming, as it were, 'a living will of God.' Seen in this light, sanctity is possible for every soul of good will; it is not impossible that a soul who leads a humble, hidden life, may adhere to the divine will as well and perhaps even better than a "great" saint who has received from God an exterior mission and has been enriched with mystical graces. The perfection of a soul may be measured by the degree to which it does the will of God, and finds its happiness in doing it. (Fr. Gabriel of St. Mary Magdalene, OCD, *Divine Intimacy*, 5)

O Lord, calm the roiling waters and whipping winds of my soul, of my overactive imagination, my frantic intellect, my brooding memory, so that I may perfectly know Thy will, to hear even its whispers. May the strength of Your presence, so recently received at Holy Mass, move me to do whatever You would have me do at each and every juncture of this day. Amen.

December 11, 2015

Another day dawns with its usual concerns and occupations. After the morning's prayer, I make Andy's lunch, then clean the house, plan dinner, feed the chickens and gather eggs. Our monthly Carmelite meeting is tomorrow so I make sure all is ready for the early morning drive. Several hours later, I head down the hill to noon Mass and then pick up the community newsletters from the printers. Prayer and activity and more prayer.

We have a beautiful Carmelite saint today, so I get to read a portion of a letter to her spiritual director in the Office of Readings, which intrigues me and heightens my desire to learn more about her than just the bare minimum.

Saint Maria Maravillas was born in 1891 in Madrid, the youngest of four children of the Spanish Ambassador to the Vatican, the Marquis, Luis Pidel. His wife, by all accounts, was a lovely, intelligent woman, known for her charity. She also had a strong devotion to Mary, under the title of Maria de las Maravillas, the patroness of the southern region of Spain where the family originated, which explains the name they chose for their daughter.

Mavi delighted in spending time with her maternal grandmother who regaled her with stories of the saints. As impressionable young children are wont to do, she took these stories to heart and, in imitation of St. Agatha, made a vow of chastity at the tender age of five. She was to recall in later years that this vow was the result of divine inspiration.

Diary of a Country Carmelite

I received the grace of vocation at the same time as the use of reason and I perceived the Lord's call so clearly that I was then as determined to be a contemplative as I am today; I have never known the slightest shadow of a doubt about it during my entire life.

She was an ordinary child in many ways despite this divine call, bubbling with joy one moment and full of mischief in her play with her siblings the next. God was preparing her through it all for a life of great service to the Church.

When Maravillas was 22 her father died and she was unwilling to leave her mother with all the cares of the family, reluctant to even mention the idea of entering the convent. She read the works of St. John of the Cross and St. Teresa of Avila and bided her time. Six years later, in 1918, her mother was the one who brought up the subject, freeing her daughter to lay bare her heart with the desire to enter Carmel, which brought her, in 1919, to present herself at the Carmel of Escorial near Madrid.

Around the same time, the Spanish King, Alphonsus XIII, erected a statue of the Sacred Heart on a hill south of Madrid in the geographic center of the country and dedicated all of Spain to the Sacred Heart of Jesus. As a young nun, Sr. Maravillas heard Jesus asking her that a convent be erected there.

In this place, I want you and the other souls chosen by my Heart to build a house in which I will take my delight. My Heart needs to be consoled. I want this Carmel to be the balm that dresses the wound opened in me by sinners. Spain will be saved by prayer.

When the mother superior had a second nun come forward with the same request, she brought the idea to the Bishop of Madrid and permission was granted to erect a convent, with Sr. Maravillas and three other nuns moving to a small house in Getafe in 1924, living here until the monastery could be built.

Spain did need saving during the turbulent years that followed. Freemasons and Communists directed a violent persecution against the Catholic Church which resulted in the enactment of anti-Catholic laws, hundreds of churches and cathedrals desecrated and burned and the wholesale murder of bishops, priests, seminarians, religious and the laity that protected them. In October 2007, Pope Benedict XVI beatified 484 of the thousands that had been killed.

As Sr. Maravillas of Jesus and her nuns prayed for Spain, spent nights in adoration and offered sacrifices, the mayhem advanced closer and closer to them. A group of armed citizens tried to attack the monastery. The Carmelites, having been enjoined by Our Lord to remain in prayer, held out for a while, faithful to their duty, until a second attack a few months later forced them to seek shelter at a nearby Ursuline convent.

The Communists now directed their anger at the statue of the Sacred Heart, which they viewed as a representation of all that Catholic Spain stood for. They tried to destroy it with any weapons at hand: bombs, bullets, hammers and finally a crane. All this could be viewed from a skylight in the convent where Sr. Maravillas, now prioress of the community, was in hiding with her nuns. Saddened, but not despairing, they moved from one place to another as the situation dictated, until the civil war ended in 1939.

Returning to the Hill of the Angels they found not only the ruins of the statue but their demolished convent. Undaunted, the nuns remained and carried on with prayer and rebuilding. More young women seeking to enter the religious life made their way up the hill. Now began the next phase in the life of our saint. New communities were founded all over Spain and old Carmelite foundations renewed and rebuilt during the 40's and 50's. In 1962, Sr. Maravillas suffered a heart attack, but this only changed the direction of her activity.

Diary of a Country Carmelite

People came to *her* now for advice and counsel. She directed more charitable work from her desk, helped to build schools and clinics, aided all the Carmelite houses in Spain and one in Ecuador and encouraged religious vocations.

Her prayer life never wavered, even in periods of great dryness, even after suffering a second heart attack in 1972. She remained the gentle superior, always present at her post until her death in 1974. The example of her holiness was seen in the short interval between her death and her beatification in 1998 and then canonization in 2003 by Pope St. John Paul II.

> We only have to live by faith and then everything becomes easy. Who could see Him acting so kindly towards us, so full of love, so attentive to our needs, and then not live for Him alone and love Him madly? What does it matter if someone does not feel faith, provided they are living every moment by it? Always live a life full of faith and trust, letting the Lord steer your boat and even sleep in it if He wants. (St. Maravillas of Jesus)

A touching story is told of a toddler in Argentina who was missing and found drowned in a muddy swimming pool just two months after Maria's beatification. His distraught mother, Alicia, calmed herself on the way to the hospital with prayer to Blessed Maria Maravillas, certain that her 18-month-old, Manuel, would be brought back to life and that he would have no physical or mental handicaps as a result of his half hour without oxygen. This miracle was accepted for the canonization of St. Maria Maravillas of Jesus.

May God be praised in all his saints! And may St. Maria Maravillas of Jesus assist us in all our activity and prayer in these dark days of unbelief and disrespect for life and virtue. So many souls are at stake.

Lord God, who drew Saint Maria Maravillas of Jesus into the secrets of the Heart of your Son, grant through her intercession and example, that we may work together for the salvation of souls, experiencing the delights of your love. We ask this through our Lord Jesus Christ, your Son, who lives and reigns with you and the Holy Spirit, one God forever and ever. Amen. (Prayer for Memorial of St. Maria Maravillas of Jesus)

December 14, 2015

It is still unusually mild for mid-December and we have had only one day with a scattering of intermittent snowflakes. Except perhaps for the ski areas, no one is complaining.

After I feed the chickens, I head west, driving in the light fog towards the Visitation Monastery for Mass. Some days it might seem hard to be so far from a Church, but having to drive for a distance is really a good extended preparation for Mass. It quiets the mind, stills the senses and puts one in a more receptive attitude for the eternal realities that are soon to be experienced. And today is one of those exceptional days when I want to banish all distractions in order to fully enter in to the celebration.

For those of us who are members of the Discalced Carmelite family, today is a Solemnity, the celebration of St. John of the Cross, known familiarly as "Our Holy Father". As befits a solemnity, Mass *is* solemn and beautiful, with the homily about St. John, Communion in the still church and an atmosphere of unhurried peacefulness in which to "commune" properly with Jesus. The day has begun well! I have no appointments to hurry back for, so I stay and pray the Office of Readings after Mass in the quiet chapel. Deo gratias!

Diary of a Country Carmelite

It seems fitting that St. John appears at the end of my year of writing about the Order's saints. Somehow, I have needed this year to become better acquainted with him, to read more of his writings and, through teaching several formation classes, to appreciate him more fully. Often one is drawn to particular saints and to others it takes a period of "warming up" in order to understand them and to truly grasp the importance of their writings and their essence.

As a Doctor of the Church and the reformer, with St Teresa, of the Carmelite Order, St. John's position is high on the pedestal of sainthood … it has just taken me longer to make my way up to where he stands.

John de Yepes began life in 1542 in Fontiveros, near Avila, Spain and due to the early death of his father and the poverty of his mother, a silk weaver, John was no stranger to hard work. As an intelligent boy and a diligent one, he found some assistance from the governor of a plague hospital. John worked at the hospital in various capacities but was also given the opportunity to attend the Jesuit college in Medina. Here he studied the classics and found his priestly vocation, choosing to enter the Carmelite Order. First came vows, then more study in Salamanca in philosophy and theology, culminating in his ordination to the priesthood in 1567.

In Medina to offer his first Mass, John encountered Teresa, several years into the reform of the nuns. Oh, happy meeting! Our persuasive, vibrant and charismatic "Holy Mother", seeing the worth of this short, young priest, soon had him collaborating with her to reform the friars, instead of leaving them for the stricter observance of the Carthusians, as he had been contemplating.

The young friar was to pack a lot into the next twenty-five years, founding colleges, serving the Order in various capacities and amassing an amazing body of written work. Bookended, though, on either side of this activity, were periods of misunderstanding, neglect and outright persecution. John was kidnapped by Carmelite friars who were opposed to his reform, imprisoned for nine months in a tiny cell and beaten regularly.

Before a daring escape, he had begun his mystical poetry—*The Spiritual Canticle.*

> *In the inner wine cellar*
> *I drank of my Beloved, and when I went abroad*
> *through all this valley,*
> *I no longer knew anything,*
> *and lost the herd that I was following.*
>
> *There he gave me his breast;*
> *There he taught me a sweet and living knowledge;*
> *And I gave myself to him,*
> *Keeping nothing back;*
> *there I promised to be his bride.*
>
> *Now I occupy my soul*
> *and all my energies in his service;*
> *I no longer tend the herd,*
> *nor have I any other work*
> *now that my every act is love.* (17-19)

In his book, *Fire Within: St. Teresa of Avila, St. John of the Cross, and the Gospel—On Prayer,* Fr. Thomas Dubay begins with some perceptive introductions to the lives of these two Carmelites. In his estimation, to fully know St. John, you must look at the essence of his being, not just his accomplishments and his body of work, although we do come to know him and his inner life deeply through his writings.

His mode of life is a likewise silent but eloquent testimony of what is indispensable for deep prayer to be given and re-ceived. (p. 33)

Diary of a Country Carmelite

Fr. Dubay says we must look at the man's traits: simple, fearless, gentle, intelligent, logical, outspoken yet soft-spoken, hard on himself but gentle with others, his appreciation for music, love of nature; clement, indulgent, benign, forgiving, *"a soul enkindled with love"*, not just his contemplative love of God, but also a very practical love that was shown to those around him.

> As we would expect, John's transformation into the divine ... showed itself in his active care for others. The dire poverty of the nuns at the Incarnation convent while he was their confessor so touched his heart that he went out to beg alms for them, and he made a point of seeking out delicacies for the ill. When his own friars were sick, the saint gave them exquisite care.... He would rise at night to check on the welfare of an ill confrere even when another friar had volunteered or been appointed to watch at the bedside.

At the end of his life, worn out by travel and activity and in declining health, John chose to live in a hostile monastery where in 1591, he died, untended and unappreciated.

Though the poetry of St. John of the Cross is considered one of the treasures of Spanish literature, it is its spiritual content that has so attracted the Catholic world over the centuries, answering these two questions: "What is the goal of man in this life?" ... Union with God ... and "How can he attain it?" John writes the science of love and if we read carefully, note the particulars and act upon them, we can ascend Mount Carmel with him. Of course, it is not an easy climb ... really the work of a lifetime, but one that is accomplished minute by minute and sacrifice by sacrifice.

> The supernatural union exists when God's will and the soul's are in conformity, so that nothing in the one is repugnant to the other. When the soul rids itself completely of what is

repugnant and unconformed to the divine will, it rests transformed in God through love. (St. John of the Cross, *Ascent of
Mount Carmel* II 5:3)

Dear St. John, hear us today and come to our aid,

> *Pour out your love upon us,
> so that we may bring love where there is none.*

Amen.

December 16, 2015

Christmas is fast approaching and as I make my list in the morning, I
see a busy day ahead of me. I start in the best way, with morning Mass,
then head back home to work on that list. Prepare some cards and a
package to mail, work for a while on an article for our little town paper,
The Blandford Bugle, and get ready for an Evangelization Committee
meeting at the parish. My aim today is to stay recollected through all
the mental activity, all the running back and forth. A brief glance at
a crucifix can help, even opening a Christmas card can serve to put
me back in the Presence of God. Or remembering the Responsorial
Psalm from Mass this morning:

> *Let the clouds rain down the Just One,
> and the earth bring forth a Savior.*

This day also has its own Carmelite to celebrate, so I can use her
life to keep me there at the side of Our Lord as well.

On the 7th of January in 1661, a little girl was born in Turin, Italy:
Marianna Fontanella, the youngest of eleven children. Her father
was Count John Donatus di Baldissero and her mother, Countess
Mary Tana di Santana, a cousin of St. Aloysius Gonzaga. She grew

to be another of those intelligent, precocious, devout children who surprise even their parents. Marianna was eight when she received her first vision and began to practice self-denial. She also heard the call to enter the religious life, and after a failed first attempt to enter the Cistercians when she was thirteen, finally joined the Carmelites of Santa Christina in 1675.

Adjusting to the life of the convent was a trial for the young girl, but she persevered through homesickness, dryness in prayer and attacks of the devil. She made her religious profession the following year as Sr. Mary of the Angels and entered fully into the contemplative life in Santa Christina. Her reputation for holiness became known in Turin and she was called upon twice when the city was in danger during attack, once in 1696 and again in 1706. Ever the humble nun, Sr. Mary of the Angels gave all the credit to St. Joseph and saw to it that Turin proclaimed him a patron. She founded another Carmel in Moncalieri, served her own community as prioress for four terms and excelled as novice mistress, teaching the young nuns to observe all the virtues with heroic effort.

Purity is so pleasing to God that his divine Son, having resolved to become man by the operation of the Holy Spirit, wished to be born of a virgin mother. We all know with what an abundance of graces and with what extraordinary purity God was pleased to adorn the body and soul of Mary. Thus he made her a dwelling worthy of the Word who was to become flesh in her chaste womb. So if we wish to induce the Incarnate God to be born spiritually in our souls, we must secure purity of conscience for ourselves. The right way to accomplish this is to banish from our hearts even the smallest faults and cultivate in them all the virtues.

O Lamb of God! How efficacious the sweetness of your love should be in softening the hardness of my heart! I detest my sins with all my strength because they are opposed to your infinite goodness. Imprint on my heart such repentance that I may prefer to die rather than ever to offend you again. (St. Mary of the Angels)

For the last twenty years of her life she was gifted with an extraordinary phenomenon; a strong, pleasant odor was present around her and even remained on objects she had touched. No doubt this further validated the opinion of the citizens of Turin that they had a saint living in their midst.

Sr. Mary of the Angels died at the age of 56 in 1717 at Moncalieri. She was beatified in 1865 and another Italian saint, Don Bosco, was given the task of writing her biography for the ceremony.

May this little Carmelite, ever constant in the love of God, help me always to remain in the Presence of our God of Love, amidst each activity and each changing of the hour.

December 17, 2015

The great and glorious *O Antiphons* begin today as we enter the Octave before Christmas. "O Sapientia ... O Wisdom" we sing in the Divine Office, and at Mass this morning, the particular readings and Gospel we know so well: the "genealogy of Jesus Christ, the son of David, the son of Abraham." I take particular delight in hearing the names, one after the other, especially as this day is the anniversary of Tim's baptism, and hearing the list of descendants puts me in mind of all families and the dignity we take on at our Baptism.

With Timothy Andrew Zozimus and all the faithful around the throne of the Lamb, we pray with the priest as he intones,

Nourished by these divine gifts, almighty God, we ask you to grant our desire: that aflame with your Spirit, we may shine like bright torches before your Christ when he comes. Who lives and reigns for ever and ever. Amen.

Most fitting words to keep in mind and take to heart as I walk out of church, and make my way up the hill to Blandford and prepare for another day at the library, another day on the pilgrimage, getting ready to welcome Wisdom and to clean my lamp so that I may shine, one day, like a bright torch before Him.

December 20, 2015

The Fourth Sunday of Advent is here already and I have planned a great pause in this day of Sunday rest to join a group of similarly oc-cupied folk in order to listen to a selection of choral works. It is late afternoon when I set out over country roads to a neighboring town to hear Novi Cantori sing works of Bach, Tallis and other composers.

What joy I have sitting in the small building, shoulder to shoulder in the wooden pews with others in the audience, all of us receptive to the beauty and harmony of the singers. *"How full I am therefore of heartfelt joy that my treasure is the alpha and omega.... With kindness deign to receive the praise and prayer of suppliants ... While all things were in quiet silence.... Furrows be glad, though earth is bare.... Thus rejoicing, free from sorrow, praises voicing, greet the morrow."*

The music becomes my prayer and I sit in interior silence to praise God in adoration.

> *Komen, du schone Freudenkrone*
> *Come sweet crown of joy.*
> *Bleib nicht lange.*
> *Do not delay.*
> *Deiner wart' ich mit Verlangen!*
> *I wait for you with longing.*

Our constant Advent prayer!

Thank you for this year, O Lord, for all its joys and sorrows. For my falling and getting up again, for all the Carmelite saints who have walked by my side over the hills and valleys of the days and months. They possess You even now as I wait in patient longing.

Wanting to prolong this quiet reverie, I stop the car on my way home in the gathering dusk to pray Vespers.

O Key of David, O royal Power of Israel controlling at your will the gate of heaven: come break down the prison walls of death for those who dwell in darkness and the shadow of death; and lead your captive people into freedom. (Canticle of Mary)

Closing my breviary, I turn the key and start the engine, following the road on the last leg of my journey home, confident of my "haven's rest" and the welcoming Guest.

Conclusion

December 25, 2015

Andy and I drove the three hours north yesterday to spend Christmas with my parents. The weather was still incredibly mild, so the travel was pleasant as we listened to Christmas music and passed through all the familiar little towns. We arrived to be welcomed with open arms, more carols and plates of food.

This morning we dress in our Sunday best and drive into the little Vermont town of Poultney for Christmas Mass. The beautiful stone church has been carefully decorated and the old wooden floor creaks in a homely way as we take our places in the front pews. There is a small congregation this morning, perhaps most of the parishoners went to last night's vigil or the Solemn Midnight Mass.

We hear the familiar, beautiful readings, sing the same dear hymns and carols and welcome the same dear Savior in His littleness and majesty into the same broken world which needs Him more than ever.

How particularly lovely to receive Communion on Christmas Day! The infant King of Love in all his defenseless littleness coming to us in the guise of a small white particle of bread. *"O Come let us adore Him, Christ the Lord!"*

Dad drives us back over the narrow, winding roads to the log cabin in the woods where we all work together to set the table and cook the Christmas brunch.

Diary of a Country Carmelite

We talk over the details of the past years, look at photographs and show Mom and Dad the pictures of their grandson and great grandsons in Alabama, the photos of Fr. Tom's Mass on this very spot in August, the shots of the family swimming in the lake and paddling the canoe. Dear memories of a family that make our days sweet.

Later in the evening I think about this past year, of all my *Country Carmelite* writings. It has been an ordinary year in many ways but punctuated by some days of great importance: my final profession in April, the celebrations of St. Teresa's 500th birthday. I "see" mental images of my own Carmelite family—the small community to which I belong—and then my focus widens as I turn to view all the Carmelite saints I have encountered this year—each one as clear as the face of a familiar friend, each one to be examined and marveled over and learned from. Each life a great gift for us and for the Church and the world, personal examples of great virtue that we can haltingly try to imitate. I give thanks to God for this year of Grace, but really for each moment, as I invoke my litany of praise.

> The whole family of Carmel in the homeland, with Mary its mother at its head, is the reason for our joy and praise to the Father on this day. We recall our brothers and sisters who once dedicated their lives to continual prayer on earth and now share in the worship of heaven. We unite ourselves spiritually to their glory, all the while journeying along the paths they traveled with courage, as they lived in obedience to Christ and followed in the footsteps of Our Lady. (*Carmelite Supplement*, introduction for feast of All Carmelite Saints)

Bibliography

Alvarez, Tomas, OCD and Domingo, Fernando, OCD. *The Divine Adventure: St. Teresa of Avila's Journeys and Foundations*. Washington, DC: ICS Publications, 2015.

Anne of St. Bartholomew. *Autobiography of the Blessed Mother Anne of St. Bartholomew*. Carmel of St. Louis, MO, 1916.

Brunot, Amadei. *Mariam, The Little Arab*. Carmel of Maria Regina, 1984.

Bush, William. *To Quell the Terror: The Mystery of the Vocation of the Sixteen Carmelites of Compiegne Guillotined July 17, 1794*. Washington, DC: ICS Publications, 1999.

De Meester, Conrad, OCD and Carmel of Dijon. *Light, Love, Life: A Look at a Face and a Heart*. Washington, DC: ICS Publications.

———. *With Empty Hands: The Message of St. Thérèse of Lisieux*. Washington, DC: ICS Publications, 2002.

Dubay, Thomas, S.M. *Fire Within: St. Teresa of Avila, St. John of the Cross and the Gospel—On Prayer*. San Francisco: Ignatius Press. 1989.

Elizabeth of the Trinity. *Elizabeth Still Speaks ... Words of the Servant of God Reported by Witnesses*. Rome, 1980.

Diary of a Country Carmelite

Gabriel of St. Mary Magdalen, OCD. *Divine Intimacy: Meditations on the Interior Life for Every Day of the Liturgical Year*. Rockford, Illinois. Tan Books, 1996.

————. *From the Sacred Heart to the Trinity: The Spiritual Itinerary of St. Teresa Margaret (Redi) of the Sacred Heart, OCD*. Washington, DC: ICS Publications, 2006.

Griffin, Michael, OCD. *God, The Joy of My Life: A Biography of St. Teresa of Jesus of the Andes*. San Francisco: Ignatius Press, 1995.

Lawrence of the Resurrection, OCD. *The Practice of the Presence of God, Critical Edition*. Washington, DC: ICS Publications, 1993.

Marie-Eugene of the Child Jesus, OCD. *I Want to See God, I am a Daughter of the Church: A Practical Synthesis of Carmelite Spirituality*. Westminster, MD: Christian Classics, 1986.

————. *Under the Torrent of His Love: St. Thérèse of Lisieux, A Spiritual Genius*. New York: Alba House, 1995.

M. Regina van der Berg, F.S.G.M. *Communion with Christ According to St. Teresa Benedicta of the Cross*. San Francisco: Ignatius Press, 2015.

Moorcroft, Jennifer. *He is My Heaven: The Life of Elizabeth of the Trinity*. Washington, DC: ICS Publications, 2001.

Muto, Susan. *John of the Cross for Today: The Ascent*. Pittsburgh: Epiphany Books, 1991.

Neyer, Maria Amata, OCD. *Edith Stein: Her Life in Photos and Documents*. Washington, DC: ICS Publications, 1999.

Rohrbach, Peter-Thomas, OCD. *Journey to Carith: The Sources and Story of the Discalced Carmelites*. Washington, DC: ICS Publications, 1966.

Rowe, Margaret. *God is Love: St. Teresa Margaret: Her Life*. Washington, DC: ICS Publications, 2003.

Ruiz, Federico, OCD. *St. John of the Cross: The Saint and His Teaching*. Darlington Carmel.

Stein, Edith. *Essential Writings, Selected with an Introduction by John Sullivan, OCD*. Maryknoll, NY: Orbis Books, 2002.

Teresa of Avila. *Collected Works*. Translated by Kieran Kavanaugh and Otilio Rodriguez, OCD. Washington: ICS Publications, 1987.

Thérèse of Lisieux. *Her Last Conversations. Translated by John Clarke, OCD.* Washington, DC: ICS Publications, 1977.

———. *Story of a Soul.* Translated by John Clarke, OCD. Washington, DC: ICS Publications, 1986.

Wilson, Christopher, Ed. *The Heirs of St. Teresa of Avila: Defenders and Disseminators of the Founding Mother's Legacy.* Washington, DC: ICS Publications, 2006.

CPSIA information can be obtained
at www.ICGtesting.com
Printed in the USA
LVHW080020260121
677508LV00018B/1138

9 780578 661506